=================Hymns, Prayers, and Songs=================

D1528492

Writings from the Ancient World
Society of Biblical Literature

Simon B. Parker, General Editor

Associate Editors

Jo Ann Hackett
Harry A. Hoffner, Jr.
Peter Machinist
Patrick D. Miller, Jr.
William J. Murnane
David I. Owen
Robert K. Ritner
Martha T. Roth

Volume 8
Hymns, Prayers, and Songs
by John L. Foster
Edited by Susan Tower Hollis

Hymns, Prayers, and Songs

An Anthology of Ancient Egyptian
Lyric Poetry

Translated by
John L. Foster

Edited by
Susan Tower Hollis

Scholars Press
Atlanta, Georgia

For
Ann, Kristi, and Rob

HYMNS, PRAYERS, AND SONGS:
AN ANTHOLOGY OF ANCIENT EGYPTIAN LYRIC POETRY
Copyright © 1995
John L. Foster

The Society of Biblical Literature gratefully acknowledges a grant from the National Endowment for the Humanities to underwrite certain editorial and research expenses of the Writings from the Ancient World series. Published results and interpretations do not necessarily represent the view of the Endowment.

Library of Congress Cataloging-in-Publication Data

Hymns, prayers, and songs : an anthology of ancient Egyptian lyric poetry /
    translated by John L. Foster ; edited by Susan Tower Hollis.
        p.   cm. — (Writings from the ancient world ; no. 8)
    Includes bibliographical references and index.
    ISBN 0-7885-0157-7 (pbk. : alk. paper) —ISBN 0-7885-0158-5
(cloth ; alk. paper)
    1. Egyptian poetry — Translations into English.   I. Foster, John
L. (John Lawrence), 1930–   .   II. Hollis, Susan T.   III. Series.
PJ1945.H45   1995
893´.1 – dc20   95-38539
                                                                              CIP

Printed in the United States of America
on acid-free paper.

Contents

v

Series Editor's Foreword

Writings from the Ancient World is designed to provide up-to-date, readable, English translations of writings recovered from the ancient Near East.

The series is intended to serve the interests of general readers, students, and educators who wish to explore the ancient Near Eastern roots of Western civilization, or compare these earliest written expressions of human thought and activity with writings from other parts of the world. It should also be useful to scholars in the humanities or social sciences who need clear, reliable translations of ancient Near Eastern materials for comparative purposes. Specialists in particular areas of the ancient Near East who need access to texts in the scripts and languages of other areas will also find these translations helpful. Given the wide range of materials translated in the series, different volumes will appeal to different interests. But these translations make available to all readers of English the world's earliest traditions as well as valuable sources of information on daily life, history, religion, etc. in the preclassical world.

The translators of the various volumes in this series are specialists in the particular languages and have based their work on the original sources and the most recent research. In their translations they attempt to convey as much as possible of the original texts in a fluent, current English. In the introductions, notes, glossaries, maps, and chronological tables, they aim to provide the essential information for an appreciation of these ancient documents.

Covering the period from the invention of writing (by 3000 B.C.E.) down to the conquests of Alexander the Great (ca. 330 B.C.E.). the ancient Near East comprised northeast Africa and southwest Asia. The cultures represented within these limits include especially Egyptian, Sumerian, Babylonian, Assyrian, Hittite, Ugaritic, Aramean, Phoenician, and Israelite. It is hoped that Writings from the Ancient World will eventually produce translations of most of the many different genres attested in these cultures: letters—official and private, myths, diplomatic documents, hymns, law collections, monumental inscriptions, tales, and administrative records, to mention but a few.

The preparation of this volume was supported in part by a generous grant from the Division of Research Programs of the National Endowment for the Humanities. Significant funding has also been made available by the Society of Biblical Literature. In addition, those involved in preparing this volume have received financial and clerical assistance from their respective institutions. Were it not for these expressions of confidence in our work, the arduous tasks of preparation, translation, editing, and publication could not have been accomplished or even undertaken. It is the hope of all who have worked on these texts or supported this work that Writings from the Ancient World will open up new horizons and deepen the humanity of all who read these volumes.

Simon B. Parker
Boston University School of Theology

Chronological Table

(after Klaus Baer)

When Dynasties overlap, each controlled different parts of Egypt. When rulers overlap within a dynasty, there was a co-regency.

I.	LATE PREDYNASTIC PERIOD	3150–3050 B.C.E.
	Narmer	
II.	ARCHAIC PERIOD	Dynasty I–II (3100–2755)
	Dynasty I	3100–2907
	Dynasty II	2907–2755
III.	OLD KINGDOM	Dynasty III–VIII (2755–2213)
	Dynasty III	2755–2680
	Djoser	2737–2717
	Dynasty IV	2680–2544
	Snefru	2680–2640
	Khufu (Cheops)	2638–2613
	Khafre (Chephren)	2603–2578
	Menkaure (Mycerinus)	2578–2553
	Dynasty V	2544–2407
	Userkaf	2544–2532
	Sahure	2532–2516
	Unis	2428–2407
	Dynasty VI	2407–2250?
	Teti	2407–2395
	Pepi I	2395–2360
	Merenrê	2357–2350
	Pepi II	2350–2260
	Dynasty VII	2250?–2230
	Dynasty VIII	2230–2213

IV. FIRST INTERMEDIATE PERIOD   Dynasty IX– XI (2213–2010)

Dynasty IX	2213–ca. 2175
Dynasty X	2175–ca. 2035
Merikare	ca. 2075
Dynasty XI	2134–1991
Mentuhotep II	2061–2010

V. MIDDLE KINGDOM   Dynasty XII–XIII (1963–1668)

Dynasty XII	1963–1782
Amenemhat I	1963–1933
Senwosret I	1943–1899/8
Amenemhat II	1901–1866
Senwosret II	1869–1862
Senwosret III	1862–1843
Amenemhat III	1843–1795
Amenemhat IV	1795–1786
Sebeknefru	1786–1782
Dynasty XIII	1782–1668

VI. SECOND INTERMEDIATE PERIOD Dynasty XIV–XVII (1720–1570)

Dynasty XIV (West Delta)	1720–1665
Dynasty XV (Hyksos)	1688–1560
Apopi	1610–1569
Dynasty XVI (Lower & Middle Egypt)	1665–1565
Dynasty XVII	1668–1570
Seqenenre Ta'o	1591–1576
Kamose	1576–1570

VII. NEW KINGDOM   Dynasty XVIII–XX (1570–1070)

Dynasty XVIII	1570–1293
Ahmose	1570–1546
Amenhotep I	1551–1524
Tuthmosis I	1524–1518
Tuthmosis II	1518–1504
Tuthmosis III	1504–1450
Hatshepsut	1503–1483
Amenhotep II	1453–1419
Tuthmosis IV	1419–1386
Amenhotep III	1386–1349

Amenhotep IV (Akhenaton)	1350–1334
Smenkare	1336–1334
Tutankhamun	1334–1325
Aye	1325–1321
Haremhab	1321–1293
Dynasty XIX	1293–1185
Ramesses I	1293–1291
Seti I	1291–1279
Ramesses II	1279–1212
Merneptah	1212–1202
Dynasty XX	1185–1070
Ramesses III	1182–1151

VIII. THIRD INTERMEDIATE PERIOD Dynasty XXI–XXV (1070–656)

Dynasty XXI	1070–946
Dynasty XXII (Libyan)	946–712
Shoshenk I (Shishak)	946–912
Dynasty XXIII (Various local Libyan Kings)	828–772
Dynasty XXIV (in Sais)	760–712
Dynasty XXV (Nubian)	772–656
Piye (Piankhy)	753–713

IX. LATE PERIOD   Dynasty XXVI–XXXI (685–332)

Dynasty XXVI (in Sais)	685–525
Psammetichus I	664–610
Dynasty XXVII (Persian)	525–404
Cambyses	525–522
Darius I	521–486
Xerxes I	486–466
Artaxerxes	465–424
Dynasty XXVIII (in Sais)	404–399
Dynasty XXIX	399–381
Dynasty XXX	381–343
Nectanebo I	381–362
Nectanebo II	360–343
Dynasty XXXI	343–332
Darius III	335–332

X. ALEXANDER THE GREAT   332–323

XI. PTOLEMAIC PERIOD	323–30
Ptolemy I (as satrap)	323–305
Ptolemy I (as king)	305–282
Ptolemy II	285–246
Ptolemy III	246–222
Ptolemy IV	222–205
Cleopatra VII	52–30

XII. ROMAN PERIOD	30 B.C.E.–330 C.E.
Augustus	30 B.C.E.–14 C.E.
Diocletian	284 C.E.–305 C.E.

Last text written in hieroglyphs: August 24, 394 C.E. (at Philae).

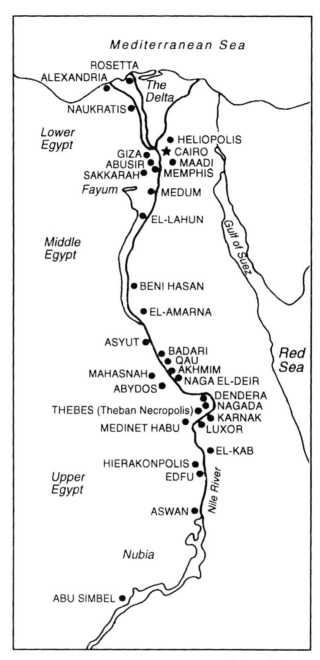

Map of Egypt
(adapted from map of sites excavated
by The Oriental Institute appearing in
Publications of the Oriental Institute 1906-1991
Oriental Institute Communications 26)

Explanation of Signs

Single brackets [ ] enclose restorations.

A row of dots (. . . . .) indicates gaps in the text or untranslatable words.

Introduction

I

The hymns and prayers of a people are its conversation with the gods. Sometimes there were many gods; sometimes, as in later religions, there was one. Over the long span of their recorded history (some three millennia), the ancient Egyptians began with many gods, usually local and often conflicting in their natures, characters, and jurisdictions. But over time, the Egyptian religion developed (however unconsciously, or consciously shaped by the theologians of the day) into one that worshiped a deity who was not only the creator but also cosmic, supreme, and preeminent among the other gods (who still existed), and god of all peoples. He was usually called Amun-Rê in the New Kingdom; but in the mind of the individual person, the best translation would be simply our word "God." The Egyptians, except for the interlude of Amarna (the monotheism of King Akhenaten in the mid-fourteenth century B.C.E.), never felt it necessary to move beyond polytheism. They did not need to reduce the richness of the many gods to a single one; for that would have done injustice to the splendor and variety of God's creation.

When an Egyptian offered, or wrote down, his hymn or prayer—his conversation with his god—the spectrum of attitudes and emotions could exhibit delight in the creation and happiness over the god's handling of human affairs; or it could express a deep longing for transcendence, a simple joy in the light of day, a thankfulness for divine protection; or it could ask for attention and help, for guidance, or for divine interference in the course of human affairs, as a supplication or petition for the god's favor—for aid in court (royal or judicial), for protection of the weak from the hands

1

of the grasping and fraudulent, for aid with studies, with advancement in a profession, or for purity of heart and power to serve the god well. In other words, the entire gamut of religious emotions and attitudes seen in the hymns and prayers of later religions—classical or Judeo-Christian—is there in the Egyptian poems.

What was the Egyptian hope? The answer to this question sets that civilization apart from all the others of its time; for the Egyptian looked forward to a happy afterlife in the presence of and under the protection of the gods. Death had to be surmounted, to be sure; and sometimes death was an enemy. But the surviving religious literature shows an almost overwhelming faith in the reality of the life beyond, of living in the presence of Osiris, worshiping him and taking communion with him eternally, while being visited nightly by the great sun-god Rê, whose beams lit the watching faces of the glorified, as he journeyed through the underworld toward his new birth at dawn. The ancient Egyptians were not a somber people, as misconception has it. Certainly life could be hard, especially for the poor. But the false impression stems more from what has been preserved from those ancient times than from temperament. Egyptians built their tombs of lasting materials because those tombs were their "houses of eternity"; and their souls would actually dwell there, as well as in the realm of the afterlife (which we would tend to call "heaven"). Buildings for use in this world, though they might have a grand purpose—a king's palace, a mayor's house, a storehouse—were built of more friable materials, primarily mud-brick; and they eventually turned to dust. So, what has endured to our own time are the stone tombs and the temples, where God was to be worshiped forever. The pyramids at Memphis, the rock-cut painted tombs in the Theban hillsides, the myriad coffins and sarcophagi, the endless mummies—all testify to an expectation of eternal life, not an obsession with death.

The time span occupied by ancient Egypt in the history of civilization was from just before the turn of the third millennium (ca. 3100 B.C.E.) down to the classical world of Greco-Roman times. Egypt flourished and was a major center of civilization from about 3100 to 1100 B.C.E. During this period it reached three peaks of culture and activity, the Old, Middle, and New Kingdoms. Only after the eleventh century B.C.E. did it relinquish its power and centrality to other, younger civilizations. Egypt endured for the better part of another millennium, but playing only a diminished role. The details of this long span can be read in the histories of Egypt, some of which appear in the bibliography at the end of this volume. The hymns, prayers, and songs were all composed in this earlier world: King David of Israel came to his throne about 1000 B.C.E.; but everything in this volume (except for poem No. 53) predates his reign by centuries, and some of it by a millennium or more. The hymns and prayers from the pyramids of Dynasties 5 and 6 were cut into the walls of kings who lived twelve or thirteen centuries before King David. And those Pyramid Texts, written to celebrate and assist in the king's resurrection, can still be seen on the walls of their tombs.

II

Ancient Egypt, like all other early civilizations, was a religious one. The secular state of the modern kind, where religions are allowed but not subsidized, was unknown. The Egyptian cosmos and the perceptions of daily life were permeated by gods. Thus, a young itinerant scholar (No. 85) could see a world filled with gods as he meditated, traveling down the Nile on the boat for Memphis; or the Ramesside "Hymn to the Nile" (No. 52) could end with "the gods are near." Only in the small body of lyric verse known as "the harper's songs" was there an overt questioning of the gods and life after death; and their purport is not clear since they appear often in conjunction with material expressing the traditional religious viewpoint. In some of the "pessimistic literature" (e.g., "The Debate Between a Man Tired of Life and His Soul") the mood will sink to despair; but the general religious scheme is not successfully questioned. The fading of a personal sense of impending deity in the modern world is a result of the scientific revolution, which for many has cleared the surrounding air of its invisible spirits. For the ancient Egyptian, the spirits—the gods—were there.

Indeed, one way to consider the ancient Egyptian's view of his deities is to think of them as one divine "stuff," some of it materialized and some of it intangible. When the creator god (whether Atum, Rê, Ptah, Aton, or Amun) began the universe, he appeared on the hillock that rose out of Chaos, bringing light and order, and fashioning the various material parts of the world. But even Chaos itself was a god—Nun. And the family created by Atum as the Nine Great Gods of Heliopolis (the Ennead)—as well as the Eight Great Gods (the Ogdoad) of Hermopolis—all come out of the same divine stuff.

The presence of this unseen divine stuff helps to explain why so many of the multiplicity of gods slowly become connected with, and then absorbed into, the natures of "stronger," more widely worshiped deities. Originally, before the unification of Egypt by Menes about 3100 B.C.E. (so the explanation goes), the country was a series of more or less autonomous smaller areas strung out along the length of the Nile, each with its local god or gods. As the political or cultural units became larger over time, the local deities came into conflict with each other, and the weaker (or the political loser) was subordinated to the stronger. The lesser god often became absorbed into the nature of the stronger, but his name would become an epithet or alternate name for the latter deity. Thus Tatenen, an ancient god of the Memphite necropolis, became an aspect or epithet of the god of Memphis, Ptah. Or Khentiamentiu, a jackal-god worshiped at Abydos, became absorbed into the nature of Osiris, as "Foremost of the Westerners."

Many of the major deities have specific personalities. Rê is always connected with the life-enhancing qualities of light and warmth; Seth is always the outsider, the antagonist; Isis is always seen with the qualities of compassion and devotion, whether to her husband or child. Amun is the "hidden god"; but he is often a god of power and conquest in his New Kingdom flowering. On the other hand, the tendency to amalgamation can be seen especially in the creator or supreme god of the pantheon. For instance, in most accounts the solar god Atum is the author of creation. But in time, as the sun-god Rê became more and more prominent, the supreme god was called Rê-Atum, though designating the single ultimate god. A similar conflation occurred in the New Kingdom as the highly visible Rê was fused with Amun, the Hidden One, into the supreme god Amun-Rê—again, a single deity with a compound name.

The gods, of course, were usually invisible, not present to human apprehension. But on occasion the god wished to appear to human beings and would become manifest to human sight. The god would materialize from the invisible divine stuff, taking a specific form or shape perceptible to human eyes. The Egyptian terms for this phenomenon are *kheperu* and *khai*. The first of these terms is variously translated in English as "manifestation," "appearance," or "form." It would perhaps be best to use the word "incarnation" for this process. The deity chooses to "embody" his invisible divine essence in a shape that can be apprehended by human eyes; and the specific form chosen is merely one of that deity's many possible incarnations. The sun-god Rê usually chooses to appear as the sun disk itself; but he can take the form of Horakhty, the Falcon of the Two Horizons, or of Atum as an old man going to his rest at the end of day. All three *kheperu* are of the sun god: Horus in the morning, Rê himself during the day, and Atum as the sun goes to rest. The *khai* of a god refers more to the splendor and glory of that appearance than to the specific figure of the god at that time.

The god could appear to human beings in various ways—through that insight which is called religious vision, or in a dream, or through a statue or icon invested with the god's power and sometimes carried in a religious procession (called "the appearance of the god"), or finally, vocally by means of an oracle. King Ramesses II, as he prays to his father, Amun, describes how the god came to save him in battle and spoke to him as if standing just behind him (No. 91). Or Pahery, the man from el Kab whose tomb gives a detailed description of the afterlife, speaks of the god who is within the human breast (No. 55). In these several ways the powers of the invisible divine realm made contact with the human world.

III

Except for the interlude of monotheism under King Akhenaten in the second half of the fourteenth century B.C.E., the religion of the ancient Egyptians was polytheistic. Their gods were legion and of all degrees of prominence and power. Some—obviously "lesser" gods—could be hunted down, butchered, boiled, and eaten in the communion meal effecting King Unas's resurrection (No. 1). Yet in the same hymn there is mention of a deity so awesome that his name cannot be named.

The multiplicity of gods has been noted; but the Egyptians did develop an orderliness to the perception of their many deities. Not all fit neatly into a specific family, pantheon, or cosmogony. The origins of several major gods have not been made clear to scholarship. Nevertheless, there is a central family of gods, and there are two major cosmogonies. The family is the Ennead, the Nine Great Gods of Heliopolis; and they represent the most widespread Egyptian view of the creation and development of the cosmos. In the Beginning, a hillock suddenly appeared out of the dark, windy, surging wateriness of Chaos (the Egyptian "Nun"); and on that hill appeared the creator god, usually called Atum. He then began the universe either through masturbation (dispensing the seeds of the cosmos), or by coughing and sneezing (expelling the breath of life), or by speaking the forms into existence. The result was the first divine couple, the god Shu (air) and the goddess Tefnut (moisture). They in turn produced Nut (sky) and Geb (earth) as the next generation. Nut and Geb were then responsible for Osiris, Isis, Nephthys, and Seth. Finally, in a distinct myth, Osiris and Isis have the child Horus.

This Heliopolitan pantheon is the result of belief in the sun-god as the ultimate deity. When Rê fused with and replaced Atum as creator god, it was he the theologians fitted into the role originally played by Atum. But when the city of Memphis was founded by Menes to begin the dynasties in the united kingdom of Upper and Lower Egypt, the god Ptah was substituted by the Memphite theologians as the creator god. Ptah spoke the universe into existence ("in the Beginning was the Word"): he had the idea in his mind; his lips expressed it; and it came to be.

The second cosmogony, centering on the Ogdoad of Hermopolis, is quite different and offers a quasi-scientific evolutionary account of the creation of the cosmos. In the chaos of Nun—the original disorder—there were four male–female pairs of deities. Nun and Naunet represent the primeval ocean; Kuk and Kauket represent darkness; Huh and Hauhet represent boundlessness, and Amun and Amaunet represent air. These divine "elements" in the original disorder set themselves in motion and created the original hillock mentioned in connection with the Heliopolitan cosmogony. At this point, with the appearance of the place where the sun-god stands to create light, the Heliopolitan cosmogony takes over.

Actually there were two major religions in ancient Egypt, the sky religion with the sun-god Rē as its focal point, and the earth religion with Osiris, god of resurrection and the blessed dead, as its central figure. These systems were probably separate at first; but the Egyptian theologians worked to harmonize them into a single body of belief whereby Rē was the creator god shining down from the heavens and Osiris was lord of the afterworld and a happy eternal life.

Outside of the myths of creation and the formation of the Ennead, the religious material concerning Rē dealt primarily with his journey across the sky in (or as) the sun disk. His incarnations as Horakhty and Atum have been mentioned. He was also thought of as a great beetle pushing the sun across the heavens much as the scarab-beetle pushed its ball of dung over the ground in Egypt. Rē would cross the sky in his Day Bark then sink below the horizon only to rise once more in the east at the next dawn. This was explained as the sun-god traversing the realm of darkness—the afterworld of the blessed dead (actually, "the ever-living")—shining upon the faces of all those Beyond and fortifying them with the rays which had shone upon them while on earth. During this night voyage—in the Night Bark—the Rē who had aged into Atum at sunset was rejuvenated to become the Divine Child or Divine Youth of the new day. During this nighttime journey, Rē and his following encountered the cosmic serpent of chaos or disorder called Apep or Apophis; and a battle between order and disorder ensued nightly. The followers of Rē had defeated Apophis each night so far; but for the Egyptians the issue had never been finally decided. Thus, the new dawn was truly a miracle, a victory of the forces of light over darkness; and the matins of the people would include a hymn of praise to the risen god renewed in splendor in the sun disk (No. 33.xxx). According to the sky religion—in a corollary that does not harmonize with the earth religion—the blessed dead joined the retinue of Rê, helping to pull his Day Bark during the daylight and drawing his Night Bark through the underworld at night. In the astral religion—a still earlier strand of religion almost lost in prehistory but impinging upon the sky religion of historical times—the dead went to be with the great gods Orion and Sothis and became stars shining in the night sky. Remnants of this subordinate theme and imagery can be seen in the Pyramid Texts.

The earth religion centered on Osiris. Like Rê, whose resurrection each dawn gave Egyptians a sense of recurrence, stability, and renewed life, Osiris, by his example, defeated death and demonstrated that all persons could similarly rise again into a new and glorious eternal life. By the New Kingdom—the last great flourishing of ancient Egyptian civilization—the individual Egyptian at death had become "an osiris." The individual emulated the example of the great god, defeating death and passing on into contentment in the next world. The myth of Osiris is seen in its most articulated form in the stele of Amenmose (No. 28).

Osiris was a good king, murdered by his jealous brother Seth (god of confusion and disorder). Seth dismembered his body and scattered the pieces throughout Egypt. Isis, the sister and wife of Osiris, mourning, searched for the pieces, reunited them, and by her power to work miracles breathed life back into his body. Because he had died, Osiris could not return to this world; but he was made king of the dead, ruler of Duat, the otherworld. He also impregnated Isis with Horus the Child. When Horus was born, Isis took him into seclusion to raise him and also to escape the pursuing Seth. When Horus came of age, Isis took him to the great conclave of the Ennead in the hall of judgment so that Horus could be protected from Seth and be awarded the land of Egypt as his inheritance from Osiris and Geb. The divine tribunal judged him "true of voice"—that is, his claims were vindicated—and Horus was given Egypt for his kingdom as the legitimate heir of Osiris.

This myth of death and resurrection fuses with another major myth of ancient Egypt—the rule of the land. For pharaoh was a god. He was given the land of Egypt to rule according to the dictates of *Maat* (a fusion of Truth, Justice, and Order); and he was truly felt to be divine by the Egyptian populace. He was the living Horus, according to the myth. But he obviously "died." Actually, he had become "an osiris" or been amalgamated to Osiris in the next world; and at his death his eldest son, the crown prince, became the new Horus, tending to his father's obsequies and assuming the leadership of the Two Lands. In this way the myth of resurrection became a powerful underpinning for the proper succession of power in Egypt. This theme also goes back in written sources to the Pyramid Texts, especially in the hymn (No. 19) in which Horus actually speaks to and performs the funerary services for his father.

<h1 style="text-align:center">IV</h1>

The gods of Egypt deserve the respect of modern readers. They need to be taken seriously for us to apprehend the richness and profundity of the ancient religion. Modern monotheistic religions too often look down on the various polytheisms as primitive and childish—pagan; and this does a disservice to what is actually there and to be savored from the ancient Egyptian sources. Part of the problem is an arrogance in living religions toward humankind's earlier attempts to comprehend deity and the cosmos; but part also is the lack of readable translations of the ancient literature. The gods become more understandable—though alien to us—when their myths, stories, rituals, and activities come down to us in a form which our imaginations can grasp. A third part of the problem is the degradation of the ancient gods, as in the belief that Egyptian deities had animal heads or were divine animals. This simply is not true. Egyptian deities were *depicted* with animal heads or as animals: their *kheperu*, their "incarnations," were represented thus so that the divinity behind the representation could be grasped by the visual imagination. But the picture or the statue was not the god, even though it could have the power of the god working through it. God is unseen; and no one knows God's origin or form (No. 33.cc), just as in the later monotheistic religions. Indeed, for the student of ancient Egyptian religion, there are major parallels to the versions of the monotheistic god in the character and attributes of the ancient Egyptian supreme god, particularly Amun-Rē of the New Kingdom. In addition, it is striking how often, as we read the individual hymn or prayer from Egypt, there is, for the worshiper, an overwhelming sense that there is no other god besides the one addressed. These poems merit close comparison with the hymns and prayers of the Judeo-Christian tradition.

<h1 style="text-align:center">V</h1>

The authors of these hymns, prayers, and songs are unknown; they have become anonymous after the millennia. Generally, only the authors of the wisdom of ancient Egypt—the maxims and moral-instruction texts—had names put to their work: Imhotep, Hordjedef, Ptahhotep, Khety, Kaires, and many others. But with the lyric poetry one must largely be content with the result alone. We can say that these authors were from priestly and courtly circles; surviving Egyptian literature is not a folk literature but rather exhibits the many intricacies of a sophisticated craft long in the learning. And the writers were all almost certainly male. There is very little overt evidence for female literacy, though surely it must have existed to some degree among the princesses at court and the priestesses in the temples.

The audience also was primarily constituted of members of the court and temple, just so long as we add the institution of the scribal schools, where young boys began their training in hieroglyphs and hieratic (the cursive form of the written language) and were introduced to the great classics of the Egyptian literary tradition. In the scribal schools (which were connected to the temples and staffed by teacher-priests) the most significant and best-loved pieces of writing were preserved, taught, studied, and copied down by the apprentice scribes. We have innumerable examples of their work, both on papyri and ostraca, usually faulty, hesitating, and with many misspellings. On one ostracon the teacher's corrections are written in red ink over the student's copy; on a papyrus poorly formed characters are properly drawn by the teacher in the margin. The "classics" were preserved because someone thought enough of them to write them down and preserve them for posterity. We have only a pitifully small portion of them; but even so, among the remains there are masterpieces. Though the author's name be lost, the hymn or prayer or song is an expression of some individual's point of view—his conception of his civilization, with its dreams and imaginations. And we can still recognize the human voice and be moved by it after four millennia and a thoroughly transformed world.

VI

The literature of ancient Egypt—its *belles lettres*, as we would say in order to distinguish this writing from more utilitarian material like historical inscriptions, letters, accounts, and such—is primarily written in verse, as poetry; and it took three fundamental forms, or fell into three basic genres—narrative, didactic, and lyric. Narrative style and structure were used for stories and myths. The didactic pieces represented a broader range and were constituted of instructional and hortatory material such as maxims, good advice, wisdom, and testaments. This genre presented the wisdom or "philosophy" of the culture. The third main genre was the lyric. This is the genre represented by the present volume, consisting of hymns, prayers, harper's songs, love songs, and a few others. The huge majority of the surviving lyric poetry of ancient Egypt was religious; and such poems venerated the nature, works, and actions of the deity (hymns) or sought help or favor from the deity (prayers), or simply sang the deity's praises. In Egypt the terminology can sometimes be confusing since the "praises" are often called "songs" rather than "hymns"—a usage that can apply both to the deity and to the divine pharaoh, who is often praised lavishly in the songs, hymns, and prayers of the New Kingdom. Two further subdivisions of the lyric genre are the harper's songs, which doubt the reality of life after death, and the love songs, our only example of a fairly extensive body of secular poetry.

Ancient Egyptian poetry has a strict and useful structure. The poems—in all genres—are written in couplets, pairs of verse lines that together make up a complete sentence or a portion of a longer compound sentence. The structure of the verse is essentially clausal: two clauses, each constituting one line of verse, make up the sentence; and of those clauses, both can be independent (a compound sentence) or one can be dependent on the other (a complex sentence). Though there are some variations (triplets and quatrains to vary the sentence and thought rhythms), this is the basis of ancient Egyptian poetic style. In addition, there is a marked attention by the author to matters of likeness and difference—in vocabulary, in grammatical patterns and clause constructions, in sound repetitions, and in thoughts. This is the "parallelism" familiar to students of biblical poetry; in Egypt it is a thousand years older. The flavor of ancient Egyptian poetic style can be hinted at by parallels to poetry in English—on the one hand, to the rhetorical couplets of the English poet Alexander Pope (but without the meter or the end rhyme) and, on the other, to the free-verse rhythms of Walt Whitman or the modernist American poets. The result is what can be called the ancient Egyptian "thought couplet."

A word should be said about this translation. The goal throughout has been what is called "a smooth literal translation." One reason ancient Egyptian literature is not well known is that so many of the current translations are *too* literal: they are intended primarily for scholars, and both continuity and overall understanding are sacrificed to word-for-word accuracy. It must be understood that these are not mistranslations; but they are not at all literary, and their style, unfortunately, rebuffs both the general reader, curious and intelligent, and specialists in other fields who are not expert in the original language. At the other end of the spectrum of translation is the literary (as opposed to literal) translation. This is where the translator attempts to reinvigorate the words in English by using all the rich armament of poetry as we know it (one assumes the translator's knowledge of the original Egyptian is accurate)—imagery, figurative language, word choice, sound repetition, rhythm, and so on. The imaginative aura of the poem—there in the original language—is *transfigured* into English. The literal translation does not attempt this, and the result is sometimes very wooden. The literary translation, on the other hand, runs the danger of creating a poem in English that was never there in the original. The smooth literal translation, as used here, attempts to be a sort of middle way.

But what translator and reader alike need to remember is that, in the mind of the ancient Egyptian author, these hymns, prayers, and songs were meant to be poems.

 **Translations**

The Transfiguration of the King
Hymns and Prayers from
The Pyramid Texts

The Pyramid Texts are the world's earliest substantial body of religious writings. They were carved and painted in the pyramid chambers of the last king (Unas) of Dynasty 5 and several of the kings of Dynasty 6 (ca. 2428–2250 B.C.E.). They comprise magical spells, exhortations, hymns, and prayers—all meant to aid the deceased pharaoh (who was, after all, a god-king) in returning to his proper sphere with the gods. As one reads the poems of this section, one is impressed by the tremendous upward thrust conveyed by the imagery; for in this early stage of ancient Egyptian religion, particularly as regards the king, the location of the afterworld (or the "horizon") is felt to be somewhere in the sky. Once his upward journey is completed, aided by the cosmic gods, the king will take his place in a renewed life with his peers for eternity.

1. The Resurrection of King Unas
[Pyramid Texts 273–274]

i

Heaven darkens, stars disappear,
    celestial bowmen are shaken, bones of the earth-gods tremble.
They are all silent, still,
    for they have looked upon Unas, the king,
Whose soul shines forth as a living god among his ancestral
        fathers;
    he is comforted by ancestral mothers.

ii

This is Unas, the King, possessor of secret wisdom,
    whose very mother knows not his hidden Name!
The splendor of Unas brightens the heavens,
    his strength the circling horizon—
Like Atum, his father, who bore him;
    and once he had borne him,
        strong was the son more than his father.
Unas's masculine powers hover about him,
    his feminine powers at his feet;
His gods are above him,
    holy serpents are at his brow,
And his uraeus-goddess precedes him:
    "Watch over his Soul! Be effective, O Fiery One!"
        The powers of Unas all are protecting him!

iii

This is Unas, the King! strong bull of heaven,
    with fury in his heart,
Who feeds on the incarnation of each god,
    who eats the organs of those
Who come—their bellies full of godly power—
    from the Island of Fire.

iv

This is Unas, the King! renewed,
    rejoining his blessed spirits.
Unas shines forth as this Great God, owner of acolyte gods;
    he sits, and his back is toward earth.

v

This is Unas, the King! judge beside One whose Name must be
        hidden
    on that day of slaughtering the firstborn.
This is Unas, the King! provider of offering meals,
    who ties the rope, himself supplying the sacrifice.
This is Unas, the King! who eats men, feeds on gods,
    possessor of tribute victims, giving swift judgment.

vi

It is Seizer of Scalp-locks, Imy-Kehau,
    who lassoes them for King Unas;
It is He of the Gleaming Head who hobbles them for him,
    driving them in to him;
It is He who oversees Blood Rites who binds for him;
    and Wanderer overpowers these divinities
To slit their throats for King Unas,
    removing their vitals—
        this is the judge Unas sends for the execution.
It is Shezemu, god of wine, who butchers them for Unas,
    cooks for him the pieces of them
        in his kettles for the evening meal.

vii

This is Unas, the King! who eats down their supernatural power,
    swallows their vital force:
Their big ones are for his morning meal,
    their middle-sized are for dinner,
Their small ones for his meal at nightfall,
    and their old men and women—sticks for his kindling!
The Great Ones of northern skies light his fires
    under the stew-pots containing them, using the thighs
        of their eldest.
Those in the heavens fly about serving him,
    stirring his kettles with legs of their women.
All the Two Heavens revolve round about him
    and the Two Banks of Egypt serve.

viii

This is Unas, the King! a great Power,
    power of powers among those with power!
This is Unas, the King! as a hawk,
    fiercest of forms of the Great Hawk.
Any he finds in his way,
    he eats him down without pausing.
His proper place is as chieftain,
    before all the eminent in the Beyond.
This is Unas, the King! a god,

older than eldest;
Thousands go about serving him,
    hundreds make offering to him.
He is given citation as "Great God"
    by Orion, the father of gods.

                    ix

King Unas has risen again, into the heavens,
    his body shines as Possessor of heaven!
He has shattered the bones of the vertebrae,
    seized on the hearts of the gods;
He has dined upon blood,
    swallowed down the fresh pieces.
King Unas is nourished by lungs of the wise ones,
    content with the life from their hearts
        and their heavenly power as well.
Upraised is the King to lap up the pieces
    which lie in the bloody broth.
The divine flesh thrives—
    their supernatural power is within him!
No more shall the honors of King Unas be kept from him—
    he has swallowed the genius of every god.

                    x

The time of King Unas, it is eternity,
    his limits, they are forever,
Through this power of his to do what he likes,
    not doing what he does not,
Within the realm of the Land of the Blessed
    for eternity and forever.

                    xi

So, their souls are deep in the body of Unas,
    their spirits subject to him,
Through this his communion consisting of gods
    cooked for the King from their bones.
So, their souls are subject to Unas,
    and their Shades are gone from their forms.
King Unas is free from them all!

Risen! Risen! Enduring! Enduring!
Evil-doers no longer have power
    to destroy the beloved house of King Unas
        among the living on this our earth
            for ever and ever more.

2. Archaic Prayers to Nut
In behalf of King Pepi
[Pyramid Texts 427–435]

i

O Nut, spread yourself out over your son, the osiris King Pepi,
    that you may conceal him from Seth.
Protect him, O Nut, he who comes to you;
        may you conceal your son, who comes to you indeed,
            may you protect this Great One.

ii

O Nut, bend over your son, the osiris King Pepi;
    protect him, O great protectress,
        this Great One who is among your offspring.

iii

Says Geb:
    O Nut, the splendor is yours,
And the power was yours from the body of your mother, Tefnut,
    before ever you were born.
May you join King Pepi to life and dominion—
    and thus he cannot die.

iv

Powerful is your heart.
    May you move back and forth in the body of your mother
        in your Name of Sky.

v

You are the daughter, powerful from her mother,
     who rose in splendor as the Bee.
May you transfigure this King Pepi within you;
     and thus he cannot die.

vi

O Great One who came to be in the sky—
     since the power is yours, and the strength is yours,
          you have filled everywhere with your loveliness.
All earth is under your sway;
     take it for your own!
You have wrapped the world in your embrace,
     all things lie within your arms;
And you have placed this King Pepi for your sake
     as an indestructible star within you.

vii

I [Rê] have separated you from Geb in your Name of Sky;
     and yet I have united all earth everywhere to you.

viii

Be high above earth!
     Yours be the zenith of your father, Shu!
          Be powerful through him!
He has loved you,
     and he has placed himself beneath you,
          underlying everything!
You have taken each god under your protection,
     providing for each his skyship
To enstar them all among the myriad lights,
     never to be driven away from you among the distant stars.
O let not King Pepi be far from you
     in your Name of Lofty One.

ix

I am Nut, the Sky, the haven at the zenith for osiris Pepi,

for the Horus beloved of the Two Lands, King Pepi,
for the King of the Sedge and the Bee, King Pepi,
For the Two Ladies, beloved of the body of gods, King Pepi,
for the Golden Horuses, King Pepi,
For the heir of Geb, and one he loves, King Pepi,
for the beloved of all the gods, King Pepi,
Given all life, stability, dominion, health, and joy,
and like Rê living forever.

3. Prayer to Nut
[Pyramid Text 350]

Hail, O Nut, far-striding goddess
who strews the greenstone, malachite, and turquoise
of the stars!
As you flourish, make King Teti flourish
just as the living reed-plant greens and flourishes!

4. Prayer of King Unas to Nut
[Pyramid Text 245]

I come to you, O Nut,
King Unas comes to you, O Nut.
I have given my father to the earth,
and I have left Horus behind me.
My wings grow strong like the wings of a falcon,
my double plume is like the hawk's.
My soul has brought me,
and my power as a god has renewed me.

[Nut answers:]

You shall take your seat in the sky amidst the stars of heaven,
for you indeed are the Lone Star, companion of Hu.
You shall look down on Osiris
as he governs the transfigured souls—

     it is you standing there high above him.
You are not down there among them,
     nor shall you ever be with them.

5. Prayer to the King to Rise Up
[Pyramid Text 373]

Oho!   Oho!
     Raise yourself up, O King Teti!
Take back your head,
     gather your bones;
Collect your limbs,
     shake the earth from your flesh;
Receive your food which does not stale,
     your drink which does not sour.

You shall stand at the gates which bar mere mortals,
     and Khentymenutef shall come to you
To grasp your hand
     and take you to the sky to Geb, your father.

And Geb will rejoice in your coming;
     and he will stretch out his arms to you,
And kiss you,
     and hold you.
And he will place you first among transfigured spirits
     and inextinguishable stars,
          and those from hidden seats will praise you.

The Great appear that they may serve you,
     the guardian gods stand guard;
Barley is threshed
     and emmer reaped for you,
Served at your monthly festivals,
     served at your mid-month feast days—
All this as ordered by your father Geb.
     Rise up, King Teti! You have not died!

6. Triumphal Hymn of Ascension
[Pyramid Text 511]

Geb shakes with laughter, Nut shouts for joy before me,
    as I myself go forth to heaven!
Sky resounds, earth trembles,
    and hail rains down for me
        as I roar out like Seth!

The guardians of sky's heritage open the gates of heaven to me
    that I may stand on Shu, the air.
For me the stars are blotted out by the fanning of gods' wings
    that I may cross the heaven like an arrow;
Sothis has three times purified the thrones,
    and I have purified myself in the pools of dawn.

The Cow who crosses the waters
    prepares my lovely pathways
To guide me toward the Great Throne which the gods made,
    which Horus created and Thoth begot.
May Isis take me, may Nephthys beget me,
    that I may surely sit on the Great Throne which
        the gods made!

Let the Dawn come to me with rejoicing
    and the gods with veneration;
Let the Horizon-dwellers come inclining their faces
    and the undying stars in obeisance.

Let me receive the altar-stone
    and attend upon the sacrifice.
I have shouldered the sky by means of life
    and sustained the earth with joy!
This right arm of mine holds the sky in dominion,
    my left sustains the earth through happiness.

Let me find myself a fare
    to summon the Guard at the Gate of Osiris—
One who hates to ferry any
    who is cannot pay passage-money.

Let me breathe in the breath of life
    that I for my own sake breathe joy,
        be overfilled with abundance of god.
And I have indeed breathed air!
    bathed by the north wind,
        content among gods!

I myself shall be skilled as the greatest of Skilled Ones
    foremost before the twin shrines of Egypt.
I shall strike with the staff
    and rule with the rod;
I shall keep the memory of me before the people
    and love of me among the gods.

Speak only that which should be spoken,
    and do not speak what is not true;
        for God detests slipshod words:
I am protected! May you not misname me!
    I am your son!
        I am the Heritor!

7. Hymn of Triumph on the King's Ascension
[Pyramid Text 509]

Sky speaks, earth trembles,
    Geb quakes, and Egypt is in uproar;
The earth has been hacked and the offering presented
    before me—who am alive, immortal!

I shall betake myself to the sky,
    sail about in the regions of life and dominion,
Traverse the heavenly waterway,
    and destroy the ramparts of Shu.

I shall betake myself to the sky
    upon feathered wings like a great bird;
I shall be cleansed within by Anubis,
    be wrapped by Horus of Abydos, embalmed by Osiris.

I shall betake myself to the sky
    among the indestructible stars;
My sister is Sothis, my guide is the morning star;
    and they hold my hand as we go toward the Field of Offerings.

I shall sit on my heavenly throne,
    with its figures of lions,
        its feet like the hooves of the Great Wild Bull.
I shall raise myself up on my throne
    in the space between the two great gods,
        my papyrus scepter in hand.

And I shall lift my hand toward the sunfolk,
    and the gods shall come to me bowing;
The two great gods shall be watchful beside them
    as they find me among the Two Enneads offering judgment.
"He is the judge of all judges!" thus they speak of me;
    and they have made offering to me among the great gods.

8. Hymn of Ascension to Rê
[Pyramid Text 407]

I, King Teti, purify myself;
    let me take my sacred place in the sky.
I, King Teti, endure;
    let my beautiful places endure.

Let me take my sacred station
    in the bow of the Bark of Rê;
The sailors rowing Rê are gods,
    and it is they who will row me also.
It is they who convey Rê about the Horizon;
    and they will convey me also about the Horizon.

My mouth is unsealed!
    My nose is unclogged!
        My ears are unstopped!
I give commands, judge contestants,
    command a god greater than I.

Rê cleanses me and protects me
from any who would do evil against me.

9. Hymn to the Risen King
[Pyramid Text 257]

"Chaos in heaven! We have seen a new thing!"
so say the primeval gods and the Ennead.
"Horus the king shines like the sun!"
thus those with divine natures greet him.
The two Enneads together serve him
who seats himself on the throne of the Lord of All.

The King takes heaven for his own,
he splits the vault of the sky.
He is guided along the ways of Khepri,
then rests alive in the West,
and those below attend him.

Then he gleams, renewed, in the East,
and the envoy of chaos comes to him bowing.
Give greeting, O gods, to the King, older than the Great One;
he is the power behind his throne.
He assumes authority, eternity is brought him,
and wisdom sits at his feet.
Praise be to him!
He has taken heaven for his own!

10. Hymn to the Risen King as Osiris
[Pyramid Text 337]

Sky shouts, earth tembles,
in terror of you, Osiris, as you accomplish resurrection!
O you dairy cows here,
you nursing cows here,

Circle about him! Weep for him!
     Shriek out for him! Mourn for him!
As he accomplishes his resurrection,
     as he arrives in the sky, among his brothers, the gods.

11. Hymn to the King as a Primordial God
[Pyramid Text 486]

Hail, primeval waters, which Shu brought forth and the
          twin springs raised,
     where Geb purified his body,
While hearts were pervaded by fear
     and minds were numb with terror!

I, King Pepi, was born in that Chaos
     before there was sky, before there was earth,
Before there were heavenly pillars, or strife,
     or the fear that came through the Eye of Horus.

I, King Pepi, am one of that body of Great Ones
     born long ago in Heliopolis,
Who are not carried off because of a king,
     not taken away before magistrates,
Not punished with death,
     not found guilty.

Such am I, King Pepi!
     I shall not be punished with death,
Not carried off because of a king,
     not taken away before magistrates.
My enemies shall not be victorious,
     I shall not be poor;
My nails shall not grow long
     nor the bones in me be broken.

Should I go down to the primal chaos,
     Osiris will raise me up, the Two Conclaves of gods
          will shoulder me,

And Rê will give me his hand to take me
wherever a god may dwell.
And should I go down into earth,
Geb will raise me up, the Two Conclaves of gods
will shoulder me,
And Rê will give me his hand to take me
wherever a god may dwell.

12. Prayer to the Celestial Ferryman
[Pyramid Text 270]

May you awake in peace,
O you of the back-turned face, in peace,
O you who watch behind, in peace,
O ferryman of the sky, in peace,
O ferryman of Nut, in peace,
O ferryman of the gods, in peace.

I, King Unas, have come to you
that you may ferry me in this ferryboat
in which you ferry the gods.
I have come to your side
just as a god might come to your side;
I have come into your presence
just as a god might come.

There are none alive who lay charges against me;
none of the dead accuses me;
No flying creature denounces me;
no four-footed beast complains.

Should you yourself fail to take me,
I will leap up
And place myself on the wings of Thoth—
and he will certainly take me across to the other side!

13. Hymn of King Unas
Ferrying across the Sky
[Pyramid Text 263]

The reed-floats of the sky are readied for Rê
    that he may cross on them to the Beyond;
The reed-floats of the sky are readied for Horakhty
    that Horakhty may cross on them to Rê;
The reed-floats of the sky are readied for King Unas
    that I may cross on them to the Beyond with Rê;
The reed-floats of the sky are readied for King Unas
    that I may cross on them to both Horakhty and to Rê.

It is well with me and with my spirit
    I am alive, together with my spirit—
My panther-skin upon me, my staff upon my arm, my scepter
       in my hand,
    I rule all those who have passed on.

They bring me those four Spirits
    who are eldest chieftains of the Sidelock-wearers,
Who dwell in the Eastern region of the sky,
    who lean upon their staffs,
That they may speak my hidden name to Rê,
    introducing me to Nehebu-kau.

Announce my entry to the floods and fields of Iaru;
    take me across the Winding Waterway;
Ferry me to the eastern side of heaven;
    ferry me to the eastern side of the sky!
My sister is Sothis
    and our child is the dawn.

14. Song of the Royal Menial
[Pyramid Text 309]

I am the menial of the gods about the Temple of Rê,
    born to Hope-of-the-Gods, she in the prow of Rê's Sun Bark.

I sit before him,
    open his boxes,
Unseal his decrees,
    seal up his letters,
Dispatch his messengers—they never weary.
    I do whatever he tells me to do.

15. Hymn to the King
As a Flash of Lightning
[Pyramid Text 261]

This is the King, who startles the heart, darling of air,
    far-stretched across the sky, a blinding light.
This is the King, a flame before the wind,
    to the limits of heaven, the ends of earth,
        until his blazing bolt is gone.
The King treads the air, strides over earth,
    kisses the waters of the ur-god's high hill.
Those at the zenith open their arms to him;
    and he stands on the heights of the eastern sky.
He has reached the end of his journey!
    This is the King, the messenger of storm.

16. Prayer of the King
As a Star Fading in the Dawn
[Pyramid Text 216]

I have come to you, O Nephthys
    I have come to you, Sun Bark of night;
I have come to you, You who are Just in the Reddening;
    I have come to you, Stars of the Northern Sky—
        remember me.

Gone is Orion, caught by the underworld,
    yet cleansed and alive in the Beyond;
Gone is Sothis, caught by the underworld,

yet cleansed and alive in the Beyond.
Gone am I, caught by the underworld,
    yet cleansed and alive in the Beyond.

It is well with me, with them,
    it is quiet for me, for them,
Within the arms of my father,
    within the arms of Atum.

17. Prayer of the King to Rê
[Pyramid Text 573]

Awake in peace, O Rê, pure one, in peace.
    Awake in peace, O Eastern Horus, in peace.
Awake in peace, O Soul of the East, in peace.
    Awake in peace, O Horus of the Horizon, in peace.
Sleep in the Night Bark,
    wake in the Day Bark,
For you are the one who watches over the gods,
    and there is no god to watch over you.

O Rê, father of King Pepi, take me to you,
    with you to live together with your mother, Nut,
Who for me will open the gates of heaven
    and throw open the doors of the firmament.
Let me come to you
    to make me live forever.
Command me to sit at your side
    or by him who brings morning from the Horizon.
O Rê, my father, command Meskhaat beside you
    to appoint a place for me
        at the Great Staircase under the sky.
Commend me to Him who has life, the son of Sothis,
    to speak for me,
        for he has promised me a seat in heaven.
Commend me to the Shining One,
    beloved and son of Ptah,
To speak on my behalf

that he maintain my offering places upon earth.
For I indeed am one from these four gods—
    Imsety, Hapy, Duamutef, and Qebehsenewef—
Who live by Truth, who hold their scepters high,
    and who watch over Upper Egypt.

I fly up! I fly up!
    —out of your grasp, mankind, and up like a bird.
In the guise of a falcon I tear my hands from your power;
    in the guise of a kite I break free of you.
I, King Pepi, am safe from any who would fetter my feet to earth;
    I am free of all who would hold me.

18. Prayer of the King
As He Offers Incense
[Pyramid Text 269]

Light fire and fire brightens;
    put incense on the fire and incense glows.

Your fragrance comes to me, O incense;
    let my fragrance come to you.
Your aromas come to me, O gods;
    let my aromas come to you.
May I be with you all, O gods;
    and may you be with me.
May I live with you, O gods;
    and may you live with me.
The King loves you, you gods;
    love him.

The wafer is working and the pellet is working
    which came from the knee of Horus.
He who had gone away comes! He comes!
    He who has risen comes! He comes!
        He who has flown up comes! He comes!

I ascend upon the lap of Isis;
    I climb up upon the lap of Nephthys;

And my father Atum takes my hand
   to bring me to those gods,
      intelligent and wise, the Imperishable Stars.

19. Prayer of the Royal Son to his Father
[Pyramid Text 606]

Rise up for me, O Father! Rise up for me, Osiris!
   It is I. Your son. I am Horus.
I have come to you to cleanse you,
   to make you pure, to bring you life,
To gather up your bones,
   to preserve your body's moisture,
      and rejoin to you what has been severed.

I am Horus, protector of his father,
   and I have struck down the one who would strike you;
I have shielded you, O father, Osiris the King,
   from him who would cause you pain.
I have come to you as envoy of Horus,
   for he has placed you, O father, Osiris the King,
Upon the throne of Rê-Atum
   that you may guide the sunfolk.

Betake yourself into the Bark of Rê
   in which the gods love to ascend,
In which the gods love to descend,
   and in which Rê rows to the Beyond.
King Merenrê has gone down into it!
   He is Rê himself!

You are seated upon the throne of Rê
   that you may pronounce the judgments of the gods.
For you indeed are Rê,
   come forth from Nut, who bears the Sun each day,
      reborn like Rê each day!

Take to yourself the birthright of your father Geb
   before the Nine Great Gods of Heliopolis.

"Who is like him?" say the two great Enneads
    who stand before the Souls of Heliopolis.
These two great and august conclaves place you—
    they who preside in the Field of Reeds—
        upon the throne of Horus, whom they fathered.

They have placed Shu on your eastern side
    and Tefnut on your west,
Nu on your south
    and Nenet on your north
To guide you toward their thrones, so beautiful and pure,
    which they had made for Rê
        when they placed him there.

O King, let them cause you to live!
    May you reach the years of Horakhty
When they created his Name
    in the heights far over the gods.
May they utter for you these chants
    as they did for Rê-Atum, who shines each day.

They have placed the King on their thrones
    as the one preceding all gods—
He is truly Rê!
    It is truly his throne!
Let this King come into being like Rê
    in this his Name of Khepri, He who Becomes.
May you arise for them like Rê
    in this his Name of the Sun.
May you turn aside from their faces like Rê
    in this your Name of Atum.

The Two Enneads rejoice, O Father,
    in drawing near to you, O Father, Osiris the King:
"Our brother comes to us!"
    say the Two Enneads, of Osiris the King, O Father,
        Osiris the King.
"One of us comes back to us!"
    say the Two Enneads, of you, O father, Osiris the King.
"The eldest son of his father comes back to us!"

say the Two Enneads, of you, O father, Osiris the King.
"Eldest son of his mother!"
    say the Two Enneads, of you, O father, Osiris the King.
"The one hurt by his brother, Seth, comes back to us!"
    say the Two Enneads, of you, O father, Osiris the King.
"Surely, Seth cannot be freed from lifting you up for eternity,
    O father, Osiris the King!"
      so say they, the Two Enneads, of you, O father,
        Osiris the King.

Raise yourself up, O father, Osiris the King!
    You are alive!

20. Hymn to Geb
[Pyramid Text 592]

O Geb, son of Shu, this is Osiris the King!
    Your mother's heart trembles for you in your Name of Geb,
      eldest of Shu, his firstborn.
Ho, Geb! This is Osiris the King!
    Join him to himself, complete him!
      For you are the great God, one alone.

Atum has given you his inheritance,
    given to you the Ennead entire,
With Atum himself among those
    his eldest twin children joined to you.
He has looked upon you, splendid, great-hearted,
    quick in your Name of Clever of Speech;
Guider of gods, you stand upon earth
    to make judgment before the Ennead.
Your fathers and mothers are more eminent than they,
    and you are powerful above any god.
Come to Osiris the King
    to protect him from his enemy.

Ho, Geb! Clever of speech, guider of gods!
    This is your son, Osiris the King!

Make him live by means of the Kingship,
    put health and prosperity in him—
For you are lord of all earth,
    powerful among the Ennead and all gods.
Be powerful,
    drive off each evil from Osiris the King,
Nor let it ever return to plague him
        in your name of the Horus who never repeats his actions—
            for you are the Spirit of all gods.
Bring them to yourself
    so that you may preserve them;
And as you cause them to live,
    cause Osiris the King to live.
        You are god, most powerful among all the gods.

The Eye came forth from your head
    as Great of Magic, the Crown of the South;
The Eye came forth from your head
    as Great of Magic, the Crown of the North.
Horus has been your companion,
    he has loved you
As you shone forth as King of Upper and Lower Egypt,
    powerful among all the gods and their Spirits.

21. Archaic Hymn
To Egypt as the Eye of Horus,
Horus being the King
[Pyramid Text 587]

Hail to you, Atum!
    Hail to you, Khepri, who came into being on his own!
You are exalted in this your Name of Height;
    You show yourself in this your Name of He who Becomes.

Hail to you, Eye of Horus,
    which he has restored with his own two hands!
He will not allow you to listen to Westerners,
    nor listen to Easterners,

Nor listen to Southerners,
    nor listen to Northerners,
Nor listen to those in the middle of the earth—
    thus you will listen to Horus.

It is he who restores you,
    he builds you up,
        he provides for you—
So do for him all that he told you
    in every place where he appears:

You shall offer him the waters which are in you
    and the waters which shall come to be in you.
You shall offer him all the trees which are in you
    and all the trees which shall come to be in you.
You shall offer him the food and drink which are in you
    and the food and drink which shall come to be in you.
You shall offer him the offerings which are in you
    and the offerings which shall come to be in you.
You shall offer up to him all that is in you
    and all that shall come to be in you;
And you shall take these offerings to him
    to every place his heart desires to be.

The gates upon you are like Iwn-mutef, the Pillar of his Mother:
    there is no opening them for the Westerners,
No opening them for the Easterners,
    no opening them for the Northerners,
No opening them for the Southerners,
    no opening them for those in the middle of the earth.

But they open for Horus!
    It is he who created them,
        raised them up;
Protected them from everything harmful
    which Seth might do against them.
For it is he who settled you
    in this your Name of Settlements.
It is he who comes and goes throughout you
    in this your Name of City.

It is he who protected you from every sort of ill
    which Seth would have done against you.

Go back, go back, O Nut!
    Geb has commanded that you go back
        in this your Name of City.

[*The King, as Horus, now repeats all the verses above to Egypt as the Eye of Horus.
The Hymn closes:*]

You shall listen to only the King. It is he who created you.
    You are not to obey the Wicked One.

22. Hymn to the Sun-God, Rê
[Pyramid Text 456]

Hail to you,
    Great One and son of a Great One!
The walls of the Shrine of the South are eager for you
    and the Shrine of the North attends you;
The doors to the windows of heaven open for you
    and the ways of the sunlight are loosened.

Hail to you,
    Unique One, who continue steadfast each day—
Horus comes! The far-strider comes!
    The Powerful One comes from the regions Beyond,
        mighty among the gods!

Hail to you,
    O Soul within that glowing fire!
Lonely one conversing with his father,
    wise one who counsels gods,
Who takes his throne in the height of heaven,
    in the place where your heart dwells at peace.
You stride across the sky according to your path,
    encompassing both North and South in your procession.

He who truly knows this spell of Rê,
    who acts upon these sayings of Horakhty—
He will be known to Rê
    and be a comrade to Horakhty.

The King is one who knows this spell of Rê,
    he follows them, these sayings of Horakhty;
Thus he will indeed be known to Rê
    and be indeed a comrade to Horakhty.
O take the King by the hand and up to heaven
    among the entourage of Rê!

23. Prayer to Atum
To Bless the King, His Pyramid, and His Pyramid City
[Pyramid Text 600]

O Atum, you who came into being high on the hill of creation
    with a blaze like the Phoenix in the Benben Shrine at
        Heliopolis—
You sneezed forth Shu,
    coughed out Tefnut;
You put your arm round about them, like the arm of a Ka;
    and your Spirit was in them.

O Atum, put your arm thus about King Neferkarê,
    about this work, about this pyramid, like the arm of a Ka,
So that the Spirit belonging to King Nerferkarê be in him,
    enduring for ever and ever.
O Atum! Place your protection over this King, Neferkarê,
    over this pyramid, over this work of King Neferkarê.
Let no evil happen to him for ever and ever
    just as you gave your protection to Shu and Tefnut.

O great Ennead in Heliopolis—
    Atum, Shu, Tefnut, Geb, Nut,
        Osiris, Isis, Nephthys, and Seth—
Children of Atum, stretch out his heart to his child
    in your Name of the Nine Bows, the Stretched Ones.

Let the King turn from you and toward Atum
    that Atum protect this King Neferkarê,
Protect this pyramid of King Neferkarê,
    and protect this work of his
From the hands of the gods, from the hands of the dead,
    and keep evil from him for ever and ever.

O Horus! This King, Neferkarê, he is Osiris!
    This work, it is Osiris! This pyramid, Osiris!
        Reveal yourself to him!
Be not far from it in its Name of Pyramid,
    completed and great in your Name of Kemwer.
Thoth has placed the gods under your jurisdiction, healthy and just,
    in the forts of Dedja and Demaa.

And Horus is your father, Osiris,
    in his Name of Iyty, He who Comes.
Horus has given the gods to you,
    he has made them mount on stone steps
        to brighten your face in the Palace of Scepters.

I I

Hymns and Prayers to Rê
The Sky Religion

The four hymns in this section, taken from a tomb at Thebes and a tomb at Memphis, both dating to the end of Dynasty 18, reflect the beliefs of the solar religion, centering on the sun-god Rê. They focus on the god's daily journey across the sky in his Sun Bark, from sunrise to sunset. Kheruef was the steward of Queen Tiye, the Great Royal Wife of King Amenhotep III. Horemheb was a military man, living during and after the Amarna heresy of King Akhenaton. He actually became pharaoh at the end of the dynasty, restoring order to the land after the Amarna interlude and providing for peaceful inauguration of Dynasty 19, the first Ramesside dynasty.

24. Hymn to the Rising Sun
[Tomb of Kheruef, TT 192]

Praise of Rê in the morning as he rises in the horizon of the sky. By the noble, mayor, confidant of Horus, Lord of the Palace, steward of the estate of the great royal wife, chief herald of the king, Kheruef, vindicated, who says:

> Hail to you!
>> Rê in your rising, concealed as Amun in your going to rest,
> You shine down from your mother's back,
>> appearing gloriously as King of the Ennead.
> Nut gives greeting at your appearance;
>> the arms of Maat protect you night and day.

You traverse the sky with joyful heart,
    and the Lake of the Two Knives is at peace;
For the Rebel is felled, his arms fettered,
    hacked with knives, his backbone broken,
Unable to walk;
      your enemies are down on their field of slaughter.

The hearts of the gods delight to see you in the Day Bark,
    and you shall have a following breeze;
      the Night Bark has destroyed him who attacked it.
You traverse your two heavens triumphantly,
    with the Nine Great Gods accompanying you;
Your mother, Nut, embraces you,
    and all is flourishing wherever you have been.

The royal scribe, chief herald of the king, steward of the great royal wife,
Kheruef, justified, who says:

Let me worship you, with your beauty in my heart,
    and may your Power grow fruitful in my breast.

25. Hymn to the Setting Sun
[Tomb of Kheruef, TT 192]

Worship of Rê when he goes to rest as one alive in the western horizon of
the sky, by the nobleman, mayor, and sole friend, who draws near his Lord,
who is in the heart of Horus, Lord of the Palace, First Royal Herald, royal
scribe, steward, Kheruef, vindicated, who says:

Hail to you, lord over eternity, Atum, great forever!
    You have joined with the horizon of the sky,
Glorious in the West as Atum of evening,
    come in your power, freed of the Enemy.

You rule the sky as Rê,
    reaching both your heavens with gladness in your heart.
You have driven away the clouds and tempest
    to go down within the body of your mother, Naunet,

While your father, Nun, gives greeting, gods of the Western
      Mountain praise,
    and those in the Underworld rejoice without ceasing,
For they see their lord of the wide-striding footsteps,
    Amun-Rê, ruler of all mankind.

Welcome in peace! O you who tread the Two Lands!
    You have gone to the arms of the Western Mountain,
And your majesty has spent the allotted time
    moored according to custom,
With the arms of your mother a protection about you
    and the guardians defeating your Enemy.

The Western Souls draw you along the path in the Sacred Land
    to brighten Underworld faces,
To hear the entreaty of him in the coffin,
    and raise up those placed on their side in the grave.

You feed on Truth beside the one who brings it,
    refresh your nostrils with what is in it,
        and are raised by it to a splendid throne.

You care for those who become gods, who arrive Yonder,
    their vital fires renewed completely by your actions,
Coming as Sundisk, Controller of Heaven,
    yet helping to rule in the realm of the dead.
You distribute your splendor throughout the underworld,
    shining brilliantly for those in the great darkness;
Those in the depths of the grave are grateful,
    and they worship you.

You reach out to them in your guise of He-Who-Awakes-Uninjured,
    who spends the night being conceived for the day,
At dawn reborn as the Divine Youth,
    the colorful Easterner amid his creation,
Who appears from his mother's womb without ceasing,
    going to rest within her until his appointed time . . . .

. . . [Kheruef] . . . [he says] . . .

Hail, you who are Rê in his rising,
  Atum going to rest,
Let me be one favored by you
  as I watch your beauty each day;
Let me take the towrope of the night-bark
  [and sail with you each night.]

26. Hymn to Rê
[From the Memphite Tomb of Horemheb]

[. . .] Horemheb, who says:

I have come to you that I may worship your splendor
  and honor your Majesty day and night.

May you take the royal scribe, Horemheb, to you in heaven,
  give him place with those honored in your following;
May his name be read during the hymns
  by the lector priest of the Lord of Abydos;
May he be in that great company
  which draws Rê to the West;
May he rise living and may he set living
  while he watches Rê's beauty;
May he be with Him in heaven and in the Underworld
  when Rê's mother gives birth each morning,
Present as one of the Ennead in Rosetau,
  glorified among the blessed spirits attending Him.

Let me enter and go forth,
  according to my wish, through the entrance of my tomb;
Let me sit in his sunlight daily,
  wandering the banks of the lake each day forever.
   Then my soul shall flutter down upon the branches
    of your trees.

The Foremost of the Westerners, Lord of the Sacred Land,
  assigned you all your duties while you were on earth,
Consumption of offerings upon the altar before the King

while you are there in the necropolis at the altar of Osiris,
And all your plans while upon earth,
    the entry to the King at the Sacred Throne,
While you are there within your gleaming heights of heaven
    beholding Rê.

Your heart will proceed to the place of your desire
    just as when you were on earth.
Your soul will be refreshed in your tomb;
    you will worship Rê from dawn until his setting,
        as you serve in his retinue.
You will take the bow-rope of the Night Bark
    as Rê proceeds in his descent Below,
With the Westerners saying, "Welcome! Welcome!"
    as he opens up the Underworld;
And then he shall dispel the darkness,
    and those who sleep will leap up at his approach.

For the hereditary prince, sole companion, master of the secrets of the
palace, fanbearer on the right of the king, supreme general of the armies,
the osiris Horemheb, justified.

27. Hymn to Rê, Thoth, and Maat
[From the Memphite Tomb of Horemheb]

My worship of Rê to please him at his rising. The nobleman, Horemheb,
says:

Hail to you, you who are glorious and creative,
    O Atum-Horakhty!
As you rise splendidly from the horizon of heaven,
    praises are yours from the mouths of everyone,
Beautiful, fresh as the youthful sun disk
    from the arms of your mother, Hathor.
Rise in splendor everywhere,
    with your heart joyful forever!

The Two Shrines of Egypt come to you in obeisance
    to offer praise at your rising.

How beautiful you are on the horizon of heaven—
    and the Two Lands are suffused with turquoise!

This is Rê-Horakhty,
    the Divine Child, heir of eternity,
        who procreated himself, bore himself by himself,
King of heaven and earth, ruler of underworld,
    chief over desert and realm of the dead;
Who came to be in the waters, drew himself forth from Nun,
    brought himself up by himself, made his offspring illustrious.

Mighty king who lights the horizon,
    the Nine Great Gods rejoice at your rising,
The whole world is happy,
    jubilant at your appearing for them.
Glorious god within his shrine,
    lord of eternity in the midst of his skyship,
The Horizon-dwellers row you,
    those in the Night Bark sail you,
The Souls of the East invoke you,
    and the Souls of the West give you praise.

You are the good god who heightens the beautiful things
      of this world,
    who tints the Two Lands gold and silver,
A youth in splendid clothing, a lord well-loved,
    mighty, unwearying,
        swift-footed, far-striding.

O ariser from eastern horizon,
    dispeller of darkness from far ends of earth,
Each eye is filled with awe
    as it offers praise at your appearing,
As it watches the Primal One with rejoicing;
    and those who accompany you kiss the earth.

You who go to rest in the western horizon,
    spreading darkness over all earth,
Light is born at your coming forth,
    earth darkens when you go down to your dwelling.

Handsome youth whom Ptah created,
   distinguished above all the gods,
You came forth as the Falcon, commander,
   with the two Serpents intertwined at your brow,
      ruling eternity, sovereign over the gods of forever.
It is you are the king, lord of the atef-crown,
   beloved, and your eyes enlighten the earth.

And you are Rê—all forms, all beings—
      all living things come to exalt you;
Your mother Nut puts awe in the Two Lands
   that they double their worship of you.
You are the primeval one, lord of eternity, great to the far end
      of time,
   who sails across the sky in the Night Bark,
      shining in splendor in the Day Bark.

By the nobleman, Horemheb, who says:

   Let me praise you, with your splendor in my eyes,
      and may your sunlight fill my breast
         as one who champions Truth
            under your Majesty, each day.

III

Hymns and Prayers to Osiris
The Earth Religion

The earth religion centered on Osiris, murdered by his brother Seth, revived by his sister-wife Isis, and installed with honor as king of the dead, Lord of the Afterlife. The theme in this strand of ancient Egyptian religious ideas is death and resurrection. The figure of Osiris embodied the Egyptian hope for a joyful eternal life, a concept unique among the ancient civilizations. The stele of Amenmose, dating to Dynasty 18 and now in the Louvre, provides the most extensive Egyptian account of the events in the story of Osiris and his son, Horus. This myth also played a profound part in the succession to the kingship of Egypt. The dead king became Osiris, and his son took the throne as the living Horus, stabilizing and protecting the divinely ruled land of Egypt. The piece from the tomb of Kheruef is an example of the shorter, more lyric rather than narrative, hymn to this deity.

28. The Great Hymn to Osiris
[Stele of Amenmose: Louvre C286]

In Praise of Osiris
By the Overseer of the Cattle of Amun, Amenmose,
Born to the Lady Nefertari.

He says:

i

Hail to you, Osiris,
   lord of eternity, king of the gods,

With myriad names, with awesome visible forms,
    with mysterious rites in the temples;
A splendid Spirit, first of the everlasting,
    with great wealth in his holy precinct;
Receiver of praise in the ancestral home of Andjeti,
    first in provisions in Heliopolis;
Who remembers clearly down in the Hall of Two Truths,
    a secretive Soul, yet lord of the underworld caverns;
Sacred in White-Wall, Soul of the Sun,
    whose earthly remains rest in Herakleopolis;
Lavish his praise from the Pomegranate Tree
    which sprang into life to lift up his Soul;
Lord of the great temple in Hermopolis,
    terrible in Hypselis;
Lord of forever, first in Abydos,
    yet distant his throne in the Land of the Dead;
Enduring his name in the mouths of the living,
    god of primeval time, belonging to all mankind—
He gave earth food, foremost of the Nine Great Gods,
    most potent Spirit among the divinities.

ii

It was for him Chaos poured forth its waters,
    for him northwind blew upstream;
Sky would make breeze for his nostrils
    so that his heart could find peace;
For his sake green things flourished,
    and for him the land brought forth its bounty;
Sky and its stars obeyed him,
    for him the great gates of heaven were opened;
Receiver of praise from southern skies,
    adored in the northern heaven;
The circumpolar stars were under his guidance,
    and the unwearying stars were his dwelling.

iii

And he went forth in peace bearing the scepter of Geb,
    and the Nine Great Gods gave him praise,
Those in the underworld kissed earth,

those in the desert bowed,
Past generations rejoiced when they saw him,
    those in the Beyond were in awe of him,
And the Two Lands united offered him adoration
    at the advent of his majesty.
Effective leader, foremost of the honored ones,
    whose jurisdiction endures, whose rule is established,
Beneficent power of the Ennead,
    kindly, loved by any who see him;
Who put awe of himself among all the nations
    so they might proclaim his name
        before all they offered him;
Whose memory is clear, whether of heaven or earth;
    unending the shouting at festival—
        rejoicing for him by the Two Lands as one.

iv

First-ranked of his divine brothers,
    noblest of the Ennead,
Who made order throughout the Two Banks,
    placed a son upon his throne,
Praised by his father, Geb,
    beloved of Nut, his mother;
With mighty hand, he threw down the rebel,
    with powerful arm, he slew his opponent,
Put the fear of himself on his enemy,
    reached the far borders of evil,
        with steady heart, he trampled their forces.

v

He inherited from Geb the kingship of the Two Lands
    when Geb saw his mastery.
He gave him his kingdom
    to guide the world to a successful future.
And he delivered this land into his hand—
    its waters, its air, its plants and pastures,
All of its walking creatures, all who fly up, all who alight,
    its creepers and crawlers, and its wild desert things—
All were presented to the son of Nut;
    and the Two Lands were pleased with it.

vi

And he rose splendid upon the throne of his father,
    like Rê when he shines from the horizon;
He put light on the face of darkness
    after he had ignited the sun with his double plume;
And he flooded the Two Lands with abundance
    like the sundisk at break of dawn.
His gleaming crown pierced the sky,
    became a brother to stars.
He was a pattern for each god,
    effective at governing;
Praised by the Nine Great Gods,
    whom the Lesser Ennead loved.

vii

His sister served as his protector,
    drove off the enemies, put a stop to the misdeeds;
Removed the Enemy by power of her spell—
    golden-tongued, her speech cannot fail,
Skilled in command,
    beneficent Isis, who rescued her brother.
She searched for him, would not give in to her weariness,
    wandered about this land in mourning,
Would not take rest
    until she had found him.
She made him shade with her feathers,
    made breeze by fanning her wings;
Danced the Dance of Last Mooring for her brother,
    tempered the weakness of Him who was weary of heart;
She received his seed, produced an heir,
    brought up the child in solitude
        (the place could not be known);
Introduced him, with his arm grown sturdy,
    into the court of Geb.

viii

And the Ennead rejoiced,
    "Welcome, Horus, son of Osiris,
Firm-hearted and true of voice,

son of Isis and heir of Osiris!"
The Tribunal of Truth assembled for him,
    the Nine Great Gods and the Lord of All;
The Lords of Truth were gathered there,
    those who turn their backs upon evil.
They sat themselves down at the court of Geb
    to offer the legacy to its rightful owner
        and the kingship to whom it belonged.
And they determined for Horus, his voice was true;
    and his father's legacy was given to him.

ix

And he went forth given the mace of Geb,
    and he took the scepter of the Two Banks,
        and the crown was firm on his head.
The earth was allotted him to be his possession,
    heaven and earth were under his care;
Entrusted to him were the people,
    and nobles, and sunfolk,
The dear land of Egypt, the middle islands;
    whatever the sundisk circles was under his governing—
The northwind, the River, the flood,
    the food-giving plants, and all vegetation.
And Nepri helped him nurture the fruits of the earth
    so that Horus might bring on abundance
        and give it to all the lands.
And everyone was glad, hearts were sweet,
    thoughts were happy, and each face showed joy.

x

They all gave praise for his goodness:
    "How sweet is the love of him, say we!
His kindliness, it has encircled the heart;
    great is the love of him in every person."
And they offered this song to the son of Isis:
"His antagonist is fallen because of his offense,
    for evil acts against the criminal;
He who commits offense, retribution comes upon him—
    as the son of Isis, who protected his father.

Hallowed be, and exalted, his name!
Majesty has taken its throne,
　　splendor endures under law;
The road is spread out, the paths are open;
　　how peaceful are the Two Banks!
Wrongdoing passes!
　　injustice is passing away!
The land is at peace under its master;
　　Lady Truth stands firm for her lord;
　　　the back is turned on iniquity!"

xi

Good health to your heart, Osiris, you who were truly good,
　　the son of Isis has taken the crown!
Adjudged to him is his father's legacy
　　within the court of Geb.
Rê spoke; Thoth wrote it down;
　　and the Divine Tribunal was pleased.
Osiris, your father Geb judged in your favor!
　　And they did just as he said.

29. Hymn to Osiris
[Tomb of Kheruef, TT 192]

Offering praise to Osiris, kissing the earth for Wennefer, by the noble-
man, mayor, sole friend of the Lord of the Two Lands, trusted by the Good
God, royal scribe, chief royal herald, steward of the great royal wife,
Kheruef, vindicated, who says:

Hail to you, [Lord] of the Sacred Land,
　　with the two horns, exalted in the atef-crown,
Greatly dreaded, master of eternity,
　　lord of Maat, rejoicing in her majesty,
Comfortable upon the great throne,
　　one the gods praise when they see him,
To whom those in the Underworld come rejoicing,
　　and [the Sunfolk kneel with] foreheads to the ground.

May your heart be gladdened in your kingship,
    your rule ensuring the throne for your son,
Horus, your successor upon earth
    after he seized the Two Lands in triumph.

The royal scribe, overseer of the estate, Kheruef, vindicated, who says:

Hail to you, Wennefer,
    son of Nut, heir of Geb,
Magnificent and majestic
    in the hearts of mankind, gods, the redeemed, and the dead,
One who inspires dread in Busiris,
    powerful in Abydos.

Let me come and go among the righteous
    who are in the following of your Majesty;
And let me feast upon the offerings of your offering table
    as is the custom of each day.

I V

Hymns and Prayers to Amun-Rê
The Apogee of Ancient Egyptian Religious Thought

Just as the New Kingdom (1550–1070 B.C.E.) was the time of greatest Egyptian political power and economic wealth—an international age in both diplomatic and cultural contacts—so also it was the time of a great development in traditional religious ideas. The heretical interlude of Akhenaton's monotheism toward the end of Dynasty 18 certainly stimulated a violent reaction in favor of traditional ideas; but there was also the development of Amun-Rê into the supreme god of Egyptian civilization. Amun-Rê was not only the creator god but also the god of all peoples and cultures in this internationalist age. He not only had supreme power, but he also cared for the individual human being as well as all the creatures of his cosmos. And he led the Egyptians to new heights of power and importance. To be sure, some of the aspects of this deity may have been incorporated from Akhenaton's god, Aton; but then Aton himself could be thought of as a reemergence of ancient traditional ideas about the god of the sun. Amun was the Hidden One (as his name implies), the invisible deity; Rê was the highly visible god in the sky, with his light and warmth. And the two deities, fused together as one supreme god, expressed the characteristics of the ultimate godhead. Religious meditations on this deity are the subject of this section: the sun hymn of Suty and Hor with its pre-Amarna hints of the Aton religion; the ritualistic and cultic hymns in the Cairo papyri, with their rather stock expressions—not good poetry but excellent for the details they convey about the worship of Amun-Rê; and, finally, the surpassing series of lyric outbursts from the Leiden papyrus, written in the time of Ramesses II, which express both the genius of a poet and the worship of a deeply religious person. The Leiden hymns give the fullest, most rounded, most vivid, and deepest portrait of Amun-Rê that we have. They are the apogee of ancient Egyptian religious thought.

55

30. To Amun as Sun God
[From the Stele of Suty and Hor]
[BM 826]

i. First Hymn: To Amun as Rê-Horakhty

The praise of Amun when he rises as Rê-Horakhty. By the Overseer of the Herds of Amun, Suty, and the Overseer of the Herds of Amun, Hor. They say:

Hail to you, Rê, beautiful each day,
    one who rises every dawn and does not cease,
        O Khepri, wearied with toil—
Your rays shine upon the face yet are not understood,
    finest gold is nothing to your brilliance;
Fashioner of yourself, you molded your own body,
    the Procreator who was never born;
One without parallel, in motion eternally,
    who oversees the million paths beneath your Image.

Your splendor is the splendor of the heavens,
    your features are more dazzling than the colors of the sky.
You ferry across above with each face watching you,
    you leave as one who hides himself from sight;
You offer yourself at dawn each day,
    the voyage which bore your Majesty has been successful;
Through the short day you cross unnumbered paths and rivers,
    and yet each moment is within your care.
Day itself passes and you go to rest;
    and you endure the hours of night as well—
You make your way by measuring them all,
    nor is there respite from your labors.

All eyes see by means of you
    and cease not when you go to rest;
You are early up to shine upon the morrow—
    it is your light opens the creatures' eyes;
And you go to rest in the Western Mountain
    that they may sleep a sleep as calm as death.

ii. Second Hymn: To Amun as Aton

Hail to you, Aton, Sundisk of day,
>who have fashioned all things and made them to live;
Great Falcon with many-hued plumes,
>Scarab who raised himself up by himself,
Who came to existence all by himself, not being born,
>Elder Horus in the midst of the sky,
Offered shouts of joy at his rising and setting,
>who created and formed the earth;
Khnum who fashioned mankind,
>who seized the Two Lands great and small;
Mut, most blessed of gods and men,
>Craftsman with kindly heart;
Great One grown weary creating them
>—and they are endless;
Brave Protector who tends his flocks,
>who is their shelter, giving them life;
Runner who measures the course,
>Khepri distinguished of birth—
His perfection raised high from the body of Nut,
>he illumines the Two Lands as the sundisk;
Primeval One who created himself,
>who oversees all his creation, alone,
Who reaches the ends of the earth each day
>in the sight of all those who walk on it;
Who shines from the sky, whose visible form is the sun
>to make seasons and months,
With heat as he wishes and cool as he wishes,
>and he makes bodies weak in order to nurture them.
Each land is glad at his rising each day
>in order to praise him.

iii. Prayer

The overseer of works, Suty, and the overseer of works, Hor, who say:

>I was in charge of your private quarters,
>>overseer of works in your shrine itself,

Made for you by your son, whom you love,
    Lord of the Two Lands, Nebmaatrê, given life.
My lord gave me the keeping of your monuments,
    for he knew that I was vigilant.
And I exercised firm control over them,
    one who did Justice according to your wish,
Because I knew that you were pleased with Maat
    and that you advanced the one who practiced it on earth.
I practiced it and you advanced me,
    doing me favors upon earth in Ipet-sut,
While I was in your following
    whenever you appeared.
I was a just man who detested wrong
    with no joy in evil words or speaking falsehood.
—As for my brother, one like myself, I always took pleasure
      in his counsel,
    for he had come from the womb with me on the same day.

The Overseers of the Herds of Amun in the Southern Harîm, Suty and Hor,
I in charge of the western side and he of the eastern side, both being in
charge of the great monuments in Ipet-Sut, foremost of Thebes, the City of
Amun.

May you give to me an old age in your City
    that I may see your splendor,
      may join the earth in the West, in the place of content.
May I be joined to the honored ones who departed in peace;
    and may you give me the sweet breeze at mooring
    and garlands on the day of festival.

31. The Cairo Hymns to Amun-Rê
[Papyrus Boulaq XVII]

In Praise of Amun-Rê,
Strong Bull in the heart of Heliopolis, authority over all gods,
the good god, well loved,
who offers life to each living thing
and to all the beautiful creatures.

i

Be praised, Amun-Rê, Lord of the Throne of the Two Lands,
    preeminent in Ipet-Sut, the Temple of Karnak,
Kamutef, Strong Bull of his Mother, first in his fields,
    far-strider, foremost in Southern Egypt,
Lord of the Medjay and ruler of Punt,
    eldest of heaven, firstborn of earth,
Lord of what is, who established all things,
    unparalleled among the gods.

Handsome Bull to the Ennead,
    authority over all deities,
Lord of Truth, father of gods,
    who created mankind, formed the creatures,
Lord of what is, grower of food-plants,
    who created pastures that cattle might live.

Handsome and mighty one fashioned by Ptah,
    divine Child handsome to love,
To whom the gods give praise,
    who created the lower and upper heavens
        as he first gave light to the world;
Who ferries across the sky in peace,
    King of Upper and Lower Egypt, Rê the Triumphant,
        authority over the Two Lands.

Powerful, majestic,
    chief who created the entire world;
Whose counsel is respected above any god,
    at whose goodness gods rejoice,
To whom followers make offering in the Shrine of the South,
    who appears in glory in the Shrine of the North;
Whose fragrance the gods love
    as he comes from Punt,
Chief of pestilence when he sends out the Medjay,
    handsome his face when he comes from the God's Land.

Whose feet the gods approach
    when they acknowledge his Majesty as their Master;
Lord inspiring fear, awesome and terrible,

overwhelming, glorious in his theophanies,
    who brings contentment, supplying abundance.

Praises to you, who created the gods,
    raised up the sky, laid the groundwork of earth.

ii

Be wakeful and be healthy, Min-Amun,
    lord everlasting, who created eternity,
Receiver of worship as foremost one in Karnak,
    with sturdy horns and handsome face,
Who wears the crown of Upper Egypt, and towering
        double plumes,
    with splendid diadem, exalted in the White Crown;
Mehenu, Nekhbet, and Buto—
    these goddesses are at his brow.

Sweet-smelling god who dwells within the palace
    with double-crown, the nemes, and the khepresh,
Handsome as he receives the atef-crown,
    beloved of the crowns of South and North;
Master of power as he takes the mace,
    lord of the scepter, bearer of the flail,
Glorious ruler, resplendent in the White Crown—
    Lord of the sunbeams, who created light!

One to whom the gods give songs of praise,
    whose arms embrace the one he loves;
Who sends the enemy chieftains to the fire,
    for his Eye fells those who rebel against him—
She strikes her spear in him who tries to drink Nun dry
    forcing the serpent-demon to cough up all he swallowed.

iii

Be praised, O Rē, Lord of Truth,
    the Amun hid in his shrine yet Lord of the gods,
Khepri, master in the sacred bark,
    who ordered that speech be when gods first appeared,
Atum, who formed mankind,

distinguished their natures, made them alive,
    made their features differ one from the other.

Who hears the prayer of the one in distress,
    is kind to whoever calls on him,
Saves the fearful man from the hand of the insolent,
    judges fairly between the wretched man and the affluent.

Lord of the Mind and Utterance, who makes his pronouncements—
    Hapy comes forth for love of him;
Pleasant and sweet, with far-reaching love—
    when he comes, mankind lives;
Who clears a path for each creature made from the
        primal Formlessness,
    who brought forth the splendor of light;
In whose beauty the gods rejoice,
    their hearts come alive when they see him.

iv

He is Rê, honored in Ipet-Sut,
    with grand theophanies in House of the Benben,
Heliopolitan, Lord of the Ogdoad,
    who has established the Sixth-day and Twice-monthly
        festivals;
Sovereign (live, prosper, be healthy) and Lord of all gods
    who gaze at him in the world Beyond,
        chief over mankind and the realm of the dead;
Hidden his name more than his offspring—
    that is, in his name of Amun, the Hidden.

v

Praises be yours, who dwell in contentment,
    lord of a joyful heart, glorious in power,
Possessor of the Crown, with towering double plumes,
    with splendid diadem, tall in the White Crown.
The sight of you is cherished by the gods—
    the Double Crown firm on your brow,
With love of you spreading throughout the Two Lands
    and your sunbeams glorious in the eye.

Mankind is beautiful at your arising,
    and beasts grow drowsy in your beams,
Your love pervades the southern sky,
    your sweetness all the northern heavens.
Your perfection takes the heart,
    your love unstrings the arm,
Your beauty of appearance makes hands useless,
    the mind forgets all else at sight of you.

Sole Perfection who made all that is,
    unique Activity who brought forth all existence,
From whose eyes mankind came forth,
    at whose command the gods began;
Who creates the pastures for the animals
    and food-plants for mankind,
Who provides for fishes in the River
    and for birds who mount the sky;
Who offers breath to all who are unborn,
    brings life to the offspring of the worm,
Provides for gnats,
    insects and fleas as well,
Supplies the fieldmice in their burrows
    and cares for all the bird-shapes in the trees.

vi

Praises to you, who created all this!
    Unique One, alone, the myriad-handed,
You who spend the night wakeful for all who must sleep,
    seeking out what is good for his creatures.
"O Amun, who established all things,
    Atum, Horus of Two Horizons—
Praises to you!" so all of them say;
    "Homage to you because you are wearied for us.
        We reverence you because you have made us."

vii

Thanks be to you from all the creatures,
    praises to you from every land
To the height of heaven, to the ends of earth,

to the depths of the Great Green Sea!
Gods bow down to your Majesty's countenance,
 to the one of surpassing power who made them;
They rejoice in the nearness of him who begot them,
 saying to you, "Welcome in peace!"

Father of fathers of all gods,
 who raised up the sky and laid down the earth;
Who created what is and fashioned existence,
 Sovereign (live, prosper, be healthy) and chief of the gods,
Let us worship your mighty power inasmuch as you have
  fashioned us;
 creation is yours for you have begotten us;
  let us offer you thanks because you are wearied for us.

viii

Praises to you, who made all things,
 Lord of Truth and father of gods,
Who created mankind and fashioned the animals,
 Lord of the Grain,
One who provides for the creatures of foreign lands,
 Amun, strong bull with the handsome countenance.

Beloved in Ipet-Sut,
 glorious in House of the Benben,
With many fillets in Heliopolis,
 who judges between the two Enemies in the great broad hall,
Chief of the Great Ennead,
 exalted, alone, without likeness,
Foremost in Ipet-Sut,
 Heliopolitan, at the head of his Ennead,
Who lives by Truth each day,
 Horizon-dweller, Eastern Horus.

For him the lands of silver and gold were created,
 and lapis lazuli for love of him,
Balsam and frankincense from the land of the Medjay,
 fresh myrrh for his nostrils;
Handsome of face when the Medjay come,
 He is Amun-Rê, Lord of the Throne of the Two Lands,

Foremost in Ipet-Sut,
    Heliopolitan, first of his harîm,
Sole king among the gods,
    with myriad names, that cannot be distinguished.

ix

One who rises from the eastern horizon,
    goes down content in the west,
Who overthrows his enemies
    according to his daily custom;
Whose eyes have raised up Thoth
    that he may bring him peace through godly power,
In whose perfection gods delight,
    whom the baboon exalts in his rejoicing.

Lord of the Night Bark and the Day Bark,
    which carry you across the floods of Chaos safely,
With your distinguished crew exulting
    as they watch You fell the Wicked One—
His limbs are cut to pieces with the knife
    and fire has eaten him,
His soul destroyed more thoroughly than his body—
    and the footsteps of this vile Antagonist are controlled.

The gods rejoice—
    Rê, the Splendid One, is safe!
Heliopolis rejoices—
    the enemy of Atum has gone down!
Ipet-Sut is safe
    and Heliopolis rejoices!
The Lady of Life, her heart is well at ease—
    the enemy of her Lord has fallen!
Gods bearing arms in the field rejoice
    and those safe in their shrines kiss the earth
        when they see his flood tide of power.

x

Power behind the gods, the Truthful, Lord of Karnak Temple—
    in your Name of Maat, Creator of Truth;

Lord of abundance, strong bull at peace—
    in your Name of Amun-Kamutef;
Who created all mankind, brought all that is into being—
    in your Name of Atum-Khepri;
Great Sky Falcon, with ornamented breast,
    with handsome face and sparkling cheek;
Perfection of creation, ringed with garlands,
    with towering crest, uraei at his brow;
To whom the hearts of all mankind are drawn,
    for whose return the sunfolk gather,
        who crowns Two Lands with glory at his Coming:—

Be praised Amun-Rê, Lord of the throne of the Two Lands,
    beloved of his city when he shines.

32. Hymn to Amun-Rê
[Credo of a High Priest of Thebes]
[Papyrus Cairo 58032]

This splendid God, Lord of all gods, Amun-Rê,
    Lord of the thrones of the Two Lands, Foremost in Ipet-Sut,
Splendid Soul who came to be in the Beginning,
    great God who dwells in Truth,
Primordial God who engendered the first gods,
    through whom every god came to be,
Most unique of the unique, who made all that is,
    who began the world back in the First Time;
Whose features are hidden, yet frequent his appearances,
    and there is no knowing how he flowed forth;
Gloriously powerful, beloved, majestic,
    mighty in his theophanies, magnificent;
Powerful Being through whose Being each Being came to be,
    who began Becoming with none but himself.

Who brought light to the world at the Creation,
    great Sundisk who brightens the sunbeams;
Who offers himself so that all men may live,
    sailing about above without being wearied;

Early riser whose ways endure,
      aged one who rises at dawn with the vigor of youth,
Reaches the ends of eternity, circles about the sky,
      traverses the place Below to brighten the world he had created.

The God who fashioned himself on his own,
      who created heaven and earth to his desire;
Eldest of old ones, most eminent of the exalted,
      greater than all the gods;
Virile Bull with the sharp horns,
      at whose great Name the Two Lands tremble;
Eternity arrives under his power,
      who reaches the far end of forever;
Great God who began Existence,
      who seized the Two Lands through his strength.

Ram-headed majesty in ancient guise
      with mien more pleasing than all other gods;
Wild lion with glowing eye,
      lord of a raging fire against his enemies;
Ancient Nun who revealed himself in his own good time
      to bring to life what came forth from his potter's wheel;
Who steps across the sky, traverses the underworld,
      at dawn repeats his practice of the day before.

Mighty in power, sacred in majesty,
      secret the contours of his bodily form;
His right eye and his left eye are the sun and moon,
      heaven and earth are united by his shining beauty;
Beneficent king who does not weary,
      strong-hearted rising or setting;
From whose sacred eyes mankind came forth,
      and the very gods are from his speaking.

Who provided food and ordered sustenance,
      created all that is, master of eternity;
Who leads forth the years,
      and yet there are no limits to his day;
Old one grown young who reaches eternity,
      aged one refashioning his youth;

With thousand eyes and hearing ears,
    who guides the millions when he shines;
Possessor of Life who offers his love,
    who encompasses the world within his care;
Who ordered forth creation, and not one thing amiss—
    nothing, of all he made, has perished.

With pleasant name and satisfying love,
    all men are early up to pray to him;
Yet terrible and awesome, great in strength,
    and every god goes in the fear of him;
Bull who grows young again, subdues his adversaries,
    whose mighty arm strikes down his enemies;
This god began the universe through his decisions,
    the Soul of the world shines forth from his two Eyes;
Invisible Spirit which took on Form,
    Khepri, the sacred one with none who knew him.

This is the King who created kings
    and united the lands by the commandments he had given;
Gods and goddesses bow to his Power
    through the greatness of his Majesty;
One who came first, he endures to the end,
    by his wisdom he began the world;
Whose Form is mysterious, there is no knowing him,
    who conceals himself from all the gods;
Who hides himself in the sundisk, there is no comprehending him,
    who masks himself even from those who emerged from him.

Fire in the sunbeams, dazzling brightness,
    whose penetrating glance pierces what is hidden;
Who spends the day watching, without tiring,
    and at dawn everybody prays to him;
Glorious when he appears within the Ennead,
    yet his figure is like every god;
Waters flow north and northwind blows upstream
    from the depths of this mysterious god
Who gives his orders to the myriad deities,
    what he has laid down shall not be removed;
With resonant voice and excellent command,

without failure in his affairs;
Who puts a term on lives, doubles the years of one he favors,
    harbors good for one who puts him in his heart,
        and builds for all eternity.

33. The Leiden Hymns
[Papyrus Leiden I 350 recto]

vi. The Gifts of the Creatures to God

Every region is in awe of you,
    even those in the Underworld praise your majesty;
Your name is exalted and your power mighty,
    Euphrates and the circling ocean dread you;
[Hapy?] makes offering to you when he arrives on earth
    and among the islands in the Great Green Sea.
Deserts and mountains descend to you,
    and [fertile] land lies in fear of you.

The people of Punt come to you,
    and the god's land blossoms for love of you;
[Nubians?] row to you bringing gums and resins
    to make your temple fragrant with aromas of festival,
And incense trees, and abundance of myrrh
    which waft to you sweet odors to mingle with your breathing;
Game, along with baked goods, foods, and honey—
    how pleasing [to the taste] such sweetness!
Oils and aromatic roots mixed with resins
    to distill the unguents which are put about your body,
[Perfumes] for your countenance,
    myrrh and genuine ladanum for your brow.

Cedar trees grow tall for you . . . . .
    to decorate your splendid bark, Userhat.
Mountains of stone flow down to you
    to elevate the gates [of your sanctuary].
Nile-ships and ships of the open sea are out on the waters
    laden and headed for your presence.

River flows north and northwind blows upstream
    to provide your Spirit with everything there is;
There is no god who is so far-reaching [as you],
    the entire [earth] is your domain.

vii. The Goddess Raiyt and Thebes

She is the one who removed the affliction from Thebes—
    Raiyt, sun-goddess, mistress of cities,
        who takes [the Two Lands] for her own;
Effective for the Lord of All,
    the holy Eye of Atum, Eye of Rê.
Who makes Thebes victorious over every city
    that she may offer this earth to the one Lord
        through her might;
Who seizes the bow, grasps the arrow—
    no fighting occurs near her because of her strength.

Each city grows great in her name—
    it is she is their Ruler, stronger than they. . . . .

[The rest is too fragmentary to translate.]

ix. Hymn at Sunrise

The Nine Great Gods are come forth from Chaos
    to gather to see you, O great of majesty—
Lord of Lords, who fashioned himself by himself,
    Lord of the Goddesses—He is the Lord!

Those who were dreaming, he shines for them all
    to brighten their faces in another of his Forms;
His eyes are gleaming, his ears are listening,
    and all his body is clothed in light.

The sky is like gold, the primeval waters are lapis lazuli blue,
    and the Southland is turquoise, as he rises among them.
The gods are watching, their temples are open,
    and people appear, to marvel and look at him.

The trees sway their bodies before him,
    turned toward the One, their arms wide with blossoms;
The scaley ones dart about in the water,
    come out of hiding for love of him;
The small beasts leap before him,
    birds dance with extended wings.

The creatures all know him at this, his loveliest moment—
    it is life to them to see him each day.
They are in his hand, stamped with his seal,
    and never a god shall open them except for his Majesty.
There is nothing created without him,
    the great God, life of the Ennead.

x. The Primacy of Thebes

Thebes is the pattern for every city;
    both waters and land came from her in the Beginning;
Then sands came to underlie fields
    and form her foundations on the heights become land;
And then faces appeared within her
    to establish each city in its true Name—
A city is named according to its purpose
    by authority of Thebes, the Eye of Rê.

Her Majesty came down as the potent and prospering Eye
    to join the world through her to the Spirit of God,
At peace, alit to dwell in Isheru
    in her form of Sakhmet, Mistress of the Two Lands.

"How mighty she is," they said about her,
    "in her Name of Waset, Dominion, the City which shall be!"
Prosperous in her Name of Wedjat, Protecting One;
    divine Eye in the Sun-disk before the face of her Lord.
Shining in glory, guiding from her high throne
    in her Name of Ipet-sut—one without equal.

Each city carries her Image
    to make itself great like Thebes.
        She is the pattern.

xx. Morning Hymn to Amun-Rê as Horakhty

How splendidly you sail the skies, Horakhty,
    accomplishing again your task of yesterday!
You who create the years, join months together—
    days, nights, and hours occur according to your footsteps;
Today you are rejuvenated far above yesterday,
    by entering the darkness you belong to day.

Sole one awake—for you detest slumber—
    everyone sleeps, yet your eyes are alert;
You reveal millions of things by your beautiful face,
    no path is devoid of you during your season on earth.
Swift-stepping, divine star and lightning flash,
    who circles the world in a moment—no secrets are kept
        from you;
Who sails across heaven, traverses the Underworld,
    the Light on each pathway which moves among men.
All are in awe of your countenance
    with mankind and gods saying, "Welcome!"

xxx. Defeat of the Enemies of Amun-Rê

The harpoon is in the Serpent, who falls to God's knife;
    rebels are given the sword by those who wreak slaughter.
He puts death in the hearts of his enemies
    so that they [groan] as outcasts forever.
He has caused that their injuries surely be lasting
    to punish his opponents, his own heart exulting.

The shrine of God is safe, the Mighty One celebrates,
    Rê is triumphant, there are no enemies of his;
The Bark of Millions of Years has good sailing,
    the divine crew rejoicing, their hearts filled with gladness.
Felled is the Adversary of the Lord of All;
    no enemy of his exists in heaven or on earth.

Sky, Thebes, Heliopolis, Underworld—
    their inhabitants delight in their deities;

For they see Him, strong in his sunrise glory,
    clad in strength and power, victor over the Evil One.
You are triumphant, Amon-Rê!
    Down are the disaffected, destroyed by the sword!

xl. The Self-Creation of God

God crafted himself, none know his nature;
    his perfect features came into being by means of
        a sacred mystery.
He shaped his own Image, fashioned himself by himself,
    beautiful Power, receptive, ingenious;
Who mingled his seed with his own bodily form
    bringing his embryo into existence from the depths
        of the mystery;
And his Form came into being, pleasing at birth—
    he finished himself to perfection, a Craftsman in forty ways.

l. The Power of God

[. . . . . .]

The Sundisk's beams streamed from the sky because of your face,
    Hapy first surged from his cavern because of your
        primeval presence;
Earth was established because of your heavenly voyaging;
    and to you, alone, belongs all that Geb nurtures.
Your Name is potent, your power preeminent;
    even mountains of iron cannot withstand your might!

Divine Falcon with extended wings,
    swift, seizing in a second whoever attacks him;
Hidden Lion with resounding war-cry,
    who hugs to himself whatever comes under his claws;
Strong Bull over his city, lion over his people,
    swishing his tail at whatever annoys him.

Earth shakes when he puts forth his cry;
    all that exists is in fear of his majesty.

He is mighty, there are none of his kind—
 he is perfection of Power, pattern for the Ennead.

lx. God's Ownership of All Creation

To him belongs the Southland as well as the North,
 for he took them, alone, for his own, in his strength;
His boundaries were set while he was still upon earth,
 wider than all earth, higher than heaven.
From him the gods request their necessities—
 and it is he who supplies from his stores.

Owner of arable fields, riverbanks, and new land—
 to him belongs each title-deed in his registry;
From beginning to end of the stretched cord
 he measures all earth with his gleaming countenance.
For him the foundation-rite was begun,
 and to him belongs the royal cubit for measuring stone.
He stretches the cord over the length of the ground,
 providing the Two Lands with his abundance of
  houses and temples.

Each city lies in his shade
 that his heart may walk about as it pleases.
Praises to him come from every dwelling,
 each holy precinct endures in its love for him.
For him they consecrate the day to festival,
 and night is spent awake amid the beauties of night;
His presence moves about over the rooftops,
 and his are the night-hymns while it is dark.

The gods receive sustenance from his Spirit:
 God is almighty, one who protects—to him they belong.

lxx. God's Mercy and Compassion

He is one who lightens misery, drives off disease,
 a physician who cures the eye without drugs,

Who opens the vision, aids the sight;
      [. . . . .]
Who rescues the one he loves though he be down
          in the Underworld
         who keeps from the hand of fate the one he would offer
            his heart.

To God belong eyes, and ears as well,
      he is a face on his every path for one who loves him;
He hears the petition of the one who cries out to him,
      instantly comes from afar to the one who summons him.
He lets life be long or wreaks havoc within it,
      offers riches beyond compare to the one who loves him.

A water-spell is Amun, his Presence is over the waters of Chaos—
      Death the Crocodile is powerless when God's name is spoken.
The winds contend, a rebel wind blows back—
      yet the departing one is content to remember God.
Words will work in the moment of terror,
      and breezes are sweet for who calls upon him,
         the Rescuer of the weary.

God is merciful, trustworthy, wise;
      his is the one who bows to him while he is there.
Effective is he above millions for one who places him in his heart;
      brave one, sole one of his Name, against hundreds of
         thousands.
Who protects the good in very truth,
      effective, who seizes the moment, with none to oppose him.

lxxx. Theogony

The Eight Great Gods were your first incarnation
      to complete this world, while you were one alone.
Your body was hidden among the oldest primordial beings,
      for you had concealed yourself as Amun from the face of
         the gods.

You fashioned your form as Tatenen, the Land,

to bring the first gods to birth back in your primeval time.
Your comeliness was honored as Kamutef, strong bull of
    his mother;
    you distanced yourself to the midst of heaven, remained as
    the sun,
Came as the fathers who engendered their sons;
    and a splendid inheritance was left for your offspring.

You began Becoming—
    there was no Being, there was no Void:
The world was from You, in the Beginning;
    all other gods came after.

[*The rest is lost.*]

xc. The Creation

All the Nine Great Gods came from your body,
    and your pattern for each was based on your bodily form.
You flowed forth first, when you began things long ago,
    as Amun, who concealed his nature from gods.

Oldest of the Old, more aged than even these;
    Tatenen who fashioned himself by himself into Ptah,
The toes of whose body were eight primordial gods;
    who rose shining as Rê from chaos that he might
        continue renewal,
Who spat out [the cosmos],
    [brought] Shu and Tefnut together by means of his Power.

Who appeared glorious on his throne, as he desired,
    by himself ruled everything through his [ability],
Joined himself to the kingship forever,
    to the end of eternity sole Lord.

Light was his incarnation in the Beginning;
    all existence was hushed in awe of him.
Then he screeched the cry of the Great Shrieker
    above the districts which he had formed, alone.

He opened speech from within the stillness;
    and he opened each eye, letting it see;
He began sounds while the world was silent—
    and his unchallenged victory-shout encircled the earth.

He gave birth to existing things that he might offer them life,
    caused all to know the paths that they should take.
Their hearts live when they see him—
    for He is the glorious One.

c. The Birth of God

Creation began with the First Occasion.
    Amun came to be first of all—and none know his means
        of inflowing.
No god became before him,
    nor was other god with him there when he spoke forth
        his form;
There was no mother to him that she might have created his nature,
    no father of his to engender the one who said, "It is I!"

He fashioned the egg of himself all by himself,
    Power whose birth was in secret, who shaped his own beauty;
Divinest of gods who came into being on his own—
    all gods came to be after he began with himself.

cc. The Forms of God: His Omnipresence

He is one whose nature is mysterious and his image dazzling,
    a god of wonders with myriad forms.
All gods boast that they come from him—
    but to exalt themselves in his beauty and holiness.

Rê himself is mingled in his bodily form,
    and he is the Fashioner dwelling in Heliopolis,
Whatever is said of Tatenen is referring to him,
    and Amun who came forth from chaos—that is God's
        image above.

Another of his forms is the Eight Great Gods;
> he engendered the primeval gods, brought forth Rê,
Completed himself as Atum, was one flesh with him;
> he is Lord of All, who began existence.

His Soul, they say, is that one above,
> and he is the one in the Underworld, first of the Easterners;
His soul is in heaven, his body in the West,
> and his visible form in Thebes to announce his appearances.

But One alone is the hidden God, who hides himself from them all,
> who conceals himself from gods, whose features cannot
>> be known.
He is farther above than heaven, deeper down than the world
>> below,
> and no gods at all can know his true nature.
No picture of him blossoms forth in the writings;
> there is no witness concerning him.
He is mysterious to the depths of his majesty—
> great beyond any perception of him,
>> mighty beyond comprehension.

An enemy dead on the instant in terror is he
> who mentions God's secret Name, with intention or not.
No god can know him by means of it—
> God is a Spirit, hidden his Name and his Mystery.

ccc. The Trinity

God is three of all gods:
> Amun, Rê, Ptah, without any others.
Hidden his name as Amun;
> He is Rê in features, his body is Ptah.
Their cities on earth endure to eternity—
> Thebes, Heliopolis, Memphis, forever.

A message is sent from the sky; it is heard in Heliopolis,
> retold in the House of the Ka to Ptah, the comely god,
Who puts it in writing in the characters of Thoth

for the City of Amun, which cares for these things.
The divine pronouncements are answered from Thebes,
    and the oracle comes forth as if from the Ennead—
All that comes from his mouth is hidden,
    so the gods administer for him what is commanded.
The message is sent: it can kill or make live—
    life and death for each one depend on it.

God reveals himself [as Amun, Rē, or Ptah,]
    [the One from] the Three united.

d. God as the Divine Warrior

The rebels against him are down on their faces,
    there are none who attack him;
The land [revives] in the midst of his enemies,
    quarrelers cannot be found before him.

Fierce lion who rends with his claws,
    drinks down in an instant the power and blood of attackers;
Strong bull, sturdy-backed, with crushing hooves
    on the neck of his enemy, tearing his breast;
Bird of prey soaring on high, seizing whoever attacks him,
    who knows how to crush his limbs and his bones.

Who takes to battle trusting his strength—
    mountains tremble beneath him when he rages;
Earth quakes when he utters the war-cry,
    all creation is in fear and terror of him.
Woe to the one who faces him, he who likes a taste of his victim—
    for he is deadly with his horns.

dc. Metaphors for God's Nature

His heart is Mind and his lips its Expression,
    his Spirit is all that exists because of his tongue;
His walking makes the twin caverns under his feet,
    and the Nile comes forth from the depression beneath
        his sandals.

His Soul is space and his thoughts the moisture,
  and he is Falcon of Twin Horizons in the midst of heaven;
His right eye is the day and his left the night,
  and it is he who guides faces down every way.

His body is Nun, and Hapy within it
  giving birth to all things and nurturing them;
His hot breeze is the breath for every nostril,
  and fate or good fortune for all are under his care.
His wife is the fertile field which he impregnates,
  his seed is the food-plants, his fluids the grain.

[He is indeed] the Great God, who engendered the primeval gods
  who are in his presence by daily custom;
Their faces are turned toward him
  as mankind and gods both say, "He is [Divine Understanding."]

dccc. Thebes, the Place of Truth

And so one moors as one of the honored, in Thebes,
  district of Truth, precinct of silence.
Worthless ones cannot enter there, the Place of Truth;
  [they cannot cross on] the ferry boat.
It [is a place] for the upright of heart;
  its ferry will not cross for the unworthy.

How delightful it is to moor within her,
  then shall one become a divine soul like the Ennead.
Thebes—She Who Is Before the Face of Her Lord—is ennobled
  from when Rê rises before her until going to rest within her,
With the mysterious Underworld concealing her Lord,
  and Debty, the god-in-his-coffin, nearby.

His Spirit is the One in the sky, his temple is Thebes,
  and [he illumines] the faces of the ennobled dead in the
    Underworld.
Sky, Thebes, Heliopolis, Underworld—
  [they rejoice in Him].

[The rest is lost.]

V

Hymns and Prayers from
The Book of the Dead
[New Kingdom and Later]

The Book of the Dead is a collection of hymns, prayers, magical spells, and
directions to help the deceased on his or her journey to the afterworld. It
was, in effect, the New-Kingdom successor to the Old-Kingdom Pyramid
Texts, the use of which had been limited to the pharaoh, and the Middle-
Kingdom Coffin Texts, a similar collection more widely disseminated but
still limited to the upper nobility. In the New Kingdom anyone who could
afford it could have a *Book of the Dead*. The Book was divided into chapters,
most with vignettes accompanying them; and the owner of the book, while
still alive, had his or her copy made to order, choosing which of the many
possible selections were particularly necessary or desirable. In the *Book of
the Dead* can be seen the characteristic fusion of the sky religion of Rê and
the underworld (earth) religion of Osiris. This is particularly evident when
Rê, after sunset, visits the kingdom of Osiris, the realm of the dead.

34. Introductory Hymn to Rê
(Papyrus of Ani)

Praise of Rê at the time of his rising from the eastern horizon of the sky, by
the osiris, scribe of the divine offerings for all the gods, Ani, who says:

> Be praised, you who are come as Khepri,
>   who came to be as creator of the gods!
> You rise and shine down from the back of your mother,

appearing gloriously as King of the Gods;
Your mother Nut raises her arms to you,
    offering greeting,
The Western Mountain receives you in peace,
    and Maat embraces you day and night.

May Rê give the power and strength of vindication,
    and a coming forth as a living Soul to see Horakhty,
To the Spirit of the osiris, the scribe, Ani,
    redeemed under Osiris.

And he says:

O all you gods of the Dwelling of the Soul,
    who judge heaven and earth in the balance,
        who give food and provisions;
O Tatenen, unique one, who created mankind;
    O Enneads of the South, North, West, and East—
Give praises to Rê, Lord of the heavens,
    the Sovereign (live, prosper, and be healthy) who created
        the gods!
Worship him in his beautiful Image
    as he rises splendid in the Day Bark.

May those who are above worship you,
    may those who are below worship you;
May Thoth and Maat write for you every day,
    and your serpent-enemy be given to the flame,
        the rebel-serpent felled, his arms fettered—
Rê has constrained his footsteps,
    the serpent-offspring are exhausted; they do not exist.

The House of the Ruler is festive,
    there is sound of rejoicing about the Great Throne,
        and the gods of Upper Egypt are glad.
For they have seen Rê appearing in glory,
    his rays flooding the lands;
The Majesty of this splendid god moves forward
    and the land of Manu unites with him.
Earth brightens with his birth each day
    once he has returned to his place of yesterday.

May you be at peace with me,
>and may I see your perfection prospering on earth!
Let me strike the Donkey, let me cut down the serpent-rebels,
>let me annihilate Apophis as he acts!
For I have seen the abdju-fish, its moment come to be;
>[and I have recognized] the bulti-fish [in its becoming,
>>while guiding] the Sun Bark on its waterway.
For I have seen Horus, helmsman,
>and Thoth and Maat with him there;
And I have seized the bow-rope of the Night Bark
>and the stern-rope of the Day Bark.

May he allow me to see the sundisk
>and glimpse the moon without ceasing every day;
And may my Soul come forth to walk about in every place it loves,
>and may my name be called
>>that I may quickly find the place of offerings;
May sustenance be given me in the presence of the Followers
>>of Horus,
>may a place be made for me in the Night Bark
>>on the day when the god ferries over;
And may I stand in the presence of Osiris in the Land of
>the Redeemed!

For the soul of the osiris, Ani.

35. Introductory Hymn to Rê
[Papyrus of Qenna]

Worship of Rê when he rises in the eastern horizon of heaven, by the osiris, the merchant Qenna, who says:

Praises to you, Rê in rising,
>Atum in your brilliant shining!
Rise! Rise! Gleam! Gleam!—
>at break of dawn appearing as King of gods.
The goddess of the double-plume has given greeting to you,
>and the Ennead worships you at its double gates
>>as you journey above, with joyful heart.

The Night Bark destroys those who attack Him,
    and the Day Bark sails upon a splendid breeze,
Rê being doubly glad,
    and your father Nun and your mother Nut appearing.
O Horakhty, come! Your sacred bark is triumphant!
    And that vile causer of strife, his head is severed;
Their hearts are alive,
    happy for their Lord at the rebel's fall.
The crew of Rê is at peace,
    and Heliopolis rejoices.

And the merchant Qenna, vindicated, says:

Let me come to you, Lord of the gods,
    Atum, Horakhty, let me rise up to Truth!
I know that your life is there:
    let me be one of your favored ones
        in [the presence] of the Great God.

One's name is called out; he is found;
    and he is commanded to [. . . .].
The steering oar of the Night Bark is grasped tightly,
    and the boat moves peacefully.
May I see Rê when he makes offering (?) on the morrow,
    his enemies felled at the place of slaughter;
May I see Horus as helmsman,
    the Oarsman working with his arms.

May I see the abju-fish, its power increasing,
    and may I glimpse the bulti-fish coming to be,
        while safely guiding the canoe on its lone waterway.

Blessed is he who is free from evil acts
    which prevent him from accomplishing the Crossing,
Who does not rend another man because of what he has,
    who does not drive a man away to take his father's property,
Who does not lie.
    [He is with] the Blessed One, Lord of Abydos.

And the merchant Qenna, vindicated, says:

Praises to you, Horakhty,
    Atum, Horus,
Khepri, the Falcon, preeminent, with particolored breast,
    with handsome face and the great double plume!
May you awake in perfection in the dawning
      with the Ennead speaking to you and all mankind
        and with shouts of praise in the evening.
Honor is yours in the Hall of Truth
      from the divine stars who go to rest weary,
        O watchful one, child who gladdens his mother each day.

Rê lives, the serpent-demon is dead!
    You are protected, your opponent is down!
May you cross the skies with life and power,
    the Day Bark moving in triumph and dignity—
Your boat joyful, your heart sweet,
    the Uraeus rising in splendor at your bow!

36. Introductory Hymn to Rê, II
(Papyrus of Qenna)

Worship of Rê when he rises from the eastern horizon of the sky, by the osiris, the merchant Qenna, vindicated, who says:

Praises to you, who rise out of Nun
    and illumine the Two Lands at your coming forth.
The Enneads in unison rejoice in you,
    the Two Ladies and the Followers have nursed you,
      O beautiful divine youth, beloved when you rise.

The common people truly live,
    Sunfolk rejoice in him;
The Souls of Heliopolis praise him,
    the Souls of Pê and Nekhen lift him high.
Baboons give veneration to him,
    and with one voice small creatures worship him.

Your Uraeus visits havoc on your enemies,
    those in the Sun Bark rejoice in you,
      your crew is victorious.

The Day Bark has united with you
    and your heart is glad, O Lord of the gods;
Those you have fashioned offer you adoration,
    with Nut deep blue beside you,
And Nun intermingling with you
    as you shoot your rays.

May you likewise illumine me
    that I may see your perfection.
I am the osiris, the merchant Qenna,
    vindicated, prospering on earth:
Let me offer worship to your beautiful countenance
    as you rise from the horizon of the sky,
And honor the sundisk when it goes to rest upon this its mountain,
    causing the Two Lands to live.

Words spoken by the merchant Qenna, vindicated, who says:

May you shine and shine!
    come forth from the chaos of Nun renewed,
        as is your daily custom,
Divine youth who came to be of himself,
    without insemination (?), come in your glory.
You have illumined the sky and the earth,
    your rays shining mingled with turquoise,
And Punt bearing aromas of your sweet fragrance
    to the tip of your nostrils;
And you shine like bronze in the sky,
    the two serpent-goddesses firm on your brow.

The Lord of the Two Lands has allotted all things,
    and all gods are honoring you.

The osiris, the merchant Qenna, vindicated.

37. Introductory Hymn to Rê
[Papyrus of Hunefer]

Worship of Rê when he rises from the eastern horizon of the sky, by the
osiris Hunefer, vindicated, who says:

Praises to you, Rê in your rising,
    Atum going to rest.
Rise! Rise! Shine! Shine!
    you who appear as king of the gods!

It is you who are lord of the sky, lord of earth,
    who created the stars above and those who are below,
        unique god who came to be in the Beginning,
Who created the earth, fashioned humanity,
    created the primeval waters, fashioned the Nile,
Who created the floods, caused those who are in them to live,
    knitted together the mountains, made men and beasts appear.

Heaven and earth give greeting to you;
    Maat embraces you day and night.
May you traverse the sky above in gladness of heart,
    with the Lake of the Two Knives at peace,
The serpent-demon felled, his arms cut away,
    and the Night Bark enjoying a following breeze.

Happy the heart of the One in his shrine,
    who appears as the Power of the sky,
The Effective One come forth from chaos,
    Rê, he is triumphant.
Divine youth, heir of eternity,
    begetter who caused his own birth,
Sole great one, who cares for creation,
    king of the world, ruler in Heliopolis,
Lord of eternity, wise in the ways of forever—
    the Ennead is joyful because of your shining.
The horizon-dweller ferries across,
    the one in the Night Bark exalts you.

Praises to you, Amun-Rê!
    resting in Maat as you ferry across above.
Everyone watches you as you grow;
    and your Majesty travels on with your rays in all faces.

There is no knowing you;
    there is no tongue to describe the likes of you.

Rather, you are unique like [. . . .]
    so that they give honor to your name;
And they swear oaths by means of you
    as the one to whom their faces turn.
You are the one who attends with your ears,
    and you see millions across the lands;
There is not an Asiatic there from whom you would draw back,
    as you watch over them, encompassed in your heart.

The day is beautiful because of your name,
    your course is far—millions upon millions of miles!
May you ferry across it in triumph,
    bound for the entering waters at the place of your desire.
You accomplish this in a little moment
    and go to rest once you have completed the hours.

By the osiris, steward of the Lord of the Two Lands, Hunefer, vindicated, who says:

Welcome, my Lord, who traverses eternity,
    whose existence is everlasting,
Welcome, O Sundisk, lord of the sunlight.
    You shine and everyone lives!
        Allow me to see the Lord of the Dawn each day.

By the osiris, the scribe, overseer of the temple of Seti I, Hunefer.

38. Introductory Hymn to Rê
[Papyrus of Nakht]

Worship of Rê by the royal scribe and general of the army, Nakht, who says:

Greetings to you, glorious and skillful,
    Atum-Horakhty,
        risen from the horizon of the sky.
Praises are yours from the mouths of everyone,
    beautiful god, renewed in the sundisk
        in the arms of your mother, Hathor.

Rise everywhere and each heart is glad forever!
  The temples of all Egypt come in homage
    to offer greeting at your rising.
Gleaming from the horizon of the sky,
  you suffuse the Two Lands with turquoise.

This is Rê-Horakhty,
  the divine youth, heir of eternity,
Who begat himself and bore himself,
  king of this earth, ruler of the underworld,
Chief over the districts of Igret,
  who came out of the primal waters,
Drew himself forth from Nun,
  nursed himself, and sanctified his birth.

O living god, who loves every living soul,
  may you shine forth splendidly as king of the gods.
Nut has offered greetings before your countenance,
  and Maat embraces you both night and day.
Joy is yours from those who attend upon you,
  they bow to the earth at your approach,.

Lord of heaven, lord of earth,
  King of Maat,
Lord of eternity, ruler everlasting,
  sovereign of all the great gods,
Living god who formed eternity,
  who fashioned the sky and set himself within it,
The Ennead rejoices when you rise,
  and earth is happy, seeing your rays.

Humanity comes forth rejoicing
  to gaze on your perfections every day
As you ferry across the sky according to your custom,
  safe and sound through your mother, Nut.
You cross the sky in gladness of heart—
  the Lake of the Two Knives is at peace,
The rebel-serpent felled, and his arms bound,
    the knife has cut through his vertebrae—
      and Rê continues on splendidly.

The Night Bark has fought through,
　　it is finished drawing you.
South, north, west, and east are praising you,
　　O primal god of earth, who came to be by himself.
Isis and Nephthys honor you,
　　they cause you to appear in glory in the two divine barks;
　　　　their arms protecting you.
The souls of the Easterners follow you,
　　the souls of the Westerners rejoice for you.

You rule all the gods,
　　receiving joy from within your chapel;
The serpent-demon is hacked for the fire,
　　and your heart is glad forever;
Your mother Nut acknowledges you,
　　you belong to your father, Nun.

39. Two Hymns to the Rising and Setting Sun
[Ch. XV, Papyrus of Ani]

Adoration of Rê in his rising from the horizon until he comes to rest in life.
Words spoken by the osiris, the scribe Ani:

i

Be praised, O Rê, in your rising,
　　Atum-Horakhty!
Let your perfections be worshiped with my eyes,
　　and let your sunlight come to be within my breast.
May you proceed in your own peace in the Night Bark,
　　your heart rejoicing in a following breeze within the Day Bark.
How delightful is the crossing of the skies among the peaceful
　　　　dead
　　with all your enemies fallen!
The unwearying stars give praise to you,
　　the indestructible stars adore you—
You who go to rest in the horizon of the Western Mountains,
　　beautiful as the Sun each day,
　　　　beautiful, enduring, as my Lord.

ii

Be praised, O Rê in your rising,
    Atum going to rest.
You are beautiful as you shine from the breast of your mother,
    appearing in glory as king of the gods!
Naunet has offered homage before you,
    and Maat embraces you both day and night.

You cross the sky in gladness of heart—
    the Lake of the Two Knives is at peace,
The rebel-serpent felled, and his arms bound,
    the knife has cut through his vertebrae.
And Rê continues on with following breeze—
    the Night Bark has destroyed those who attacked him.
Southerners and Northerners draw you along
    while Westerners and Easterners give praise.

Primal deity who brought forth the forms of being, who raised
      his voice
    when the earth was flooded with silence;
Sole One who came to be in the midst of the sky
    before there was ground or mountains;
Shepherd, sole Lord, who created all that exists,
    whose tongue fashioned the Ennead of his gods;
Who nursed the seeds of all that is in the waters
    whence you emerged on the bank of the Lake of Horus.

Let me breathe the breath which comes from your nostrils
    and the northwind which comes from your mother!
May you transfigure my spirit,
    make sacred the osiris, my soul!
Be praised in triumph, O Lord of the gods,
    be exalted in the midst of your wonders!
      Pour your rays over my breast like the daylight!

The osiris and scribe of accounts of the ritual offerings for all the gods, overseer of the Two Granaries of the lords of the district of Ta-wer, the genuine royal scribe, whom he loves, Ani, vindicated and triumphant.

40. Hymns to the Rising Sun
[Ch. XV, Papyrus Ani]

i

Praise of Rê at dawn when he rises from the eastern horizon of the sky along with those who are in his following, by the osiris, Ani, vindicated, who says:

> Hail, O Sundisk, lord of the sunbeams,
>> who rises from the horizon each day!
> May you glow in the face of Ani, the vindicated;
>> let him adore you at daybreak,
>>> let him please you at evening!
> May the Soul of the osiris Ani, the vindicated,
>> go forth with you to the sky
> That he may command in the Day Bark,
>> endure in the Night Bark,
>>> and join the indestructible, unwearying stars!
> The osiris Ani being triumphant and vindicated—
>> may he say that he honors his lord, the Lord of eternity.

ii

> Praises to you, O Horus of Two Horizons,
>> Khepri, that is, who came to be by himself.
> How beautiful is your rising from the horizon
>> to illumine the Two Lands with your sunlight,
> With all the gods rejoicing
>> when they see you as king of the heavens;
> With the Lady of the Uraeus firm on your head,
>> the goddess of Upper and Lower Egypt at your brow—
>>> she has taken her place before you;
> With Thoth moving ahead of your sacred bark
>> destroying all your enemies;
> With those in the underworld come forth to greet you,
>> to see this beautiful sight.

> I have come to you, and I am with you,
>> to see your sundisk each day:
> Let me not be prevented, let me not be turned back,

let my limbs be renewed at seeing your perfection,
Just like all those you have honored,
    for I am one you treasured on earth.
Now I have reached the land of eternity,
    I have joined the land of everlasting;
        and you indeed have commanded it for me, my Lord.

iii

Spoken by the osiris Ani, vindicated and triumphant, who says:

Praises be to you, when you rise from your horizon as Rê,
    at peace in Maat as you cross the sky,
With every face watching you
    until you depart, concealed from their sight.
You offer yourself at the dawn and the darkening of day:
    how fortunate they are who voyage with your Majesty!
Your beams shine in the face, but there is no understanding them;
    the brilliance of fine gold is nothing to your own.

The realms of the gods have been described in the writings,
    and the highlands of Punt can be explored;
But you yourself were concealed when you created,
    one alone, except for your Word.

Your first incarnation was Nun, the primal ocean,
    and he would make his movements follow yours;
Nor does he make a pause—just like your Majesty;
    the day is short, the journey far,
Millions upon millions of miles,
    yet just a little moment and you have accomplished it.

You have gone to rest,
    and, same as in the day, you spend the hours of night,
Dividing them,
    completing them according to your custom.
At daybreak, you present yourself once more as Rê,
    rising in glory over the horizon.

iv

The osiris, the scribe Ani, vindicated, who speaks:

May he worship you in your shining,
    let him speak to you at your rising.

May you be early up for the worship of your visible forms,
    may you shine in the wealth of your perfections, O Traveller.
You fashioned your own form, without birth,
    as Rê who shines down from the sky.

O let me reach the heaven of eternity,
    the district of those who are honored;
May I join the transfigured dead, most favored in the city of the
        dead;
    and let me go forth with them to see your perfection.
May you shine in the evening
    after you have traversed your mother, Naunet;
May you turn my face to the West,
    my arms in adoration at your going to rest as one living.

For you indeed created eternity!
    Be praised, as you go to rest in Nun.
Let me place you in my heart,
    O you without weariness, more divine than the gods!

v

The osiris Ani, vindicated, who says:

Praises to you, who rise golden
    lighting the Two Lands with day because of your birth.
Your mother brought you forth upon her hand,
    and you illumined all the sundisk circles—
The great Enlightener who rose shining out of Nun,
    who marshals followers from out the primal waters,
Who makes the districts of the cities rich with festivals,
    lord of processions,
Lord who protects through your perfections—
    your Spirit blossoms forth in food and sustenance;
Greatly to be feared, strongest of the powerful,
    who arms your throne against the evildoers;
Awesome in appearance in the Night Bark,
    your greatness is far-reaching in the Day Bark.

May you transfigure the osiris Ani, rescued from the grave,
    and may you let him be there in the West;
You who are free of evil,
    may you forgive wrongdoing.
Place me as a blessed spirit among your transfigured ones
    that I may join the Spirits in the Sacred Land
And sail about the Field of Reeds
    according to command from Him, the Lord of Joy.

By the osiris, the scribe Ani, vindicated.

vi

[God answers:]

You shall go forth to the sky,
    travel across the firmament, be brother to the stars.
Praises are offered for you in the sunship,
    and you are given summons to the Day Bark.
You shall see Rê within his shrine,
    and you shall give his sundisk pleasure every day.

For you have seen the bulti-fish in all its forms upon the
        Sea of Turquoise,
    and you have seen the abdju-fish—its time has come—
The evil one is fallen as foretold,
    for I have had the knife cut through his vertebrae.
And Rê shall journey on with following breeze,
    the Night Bark destroying him who would attack it,
        the crew of Rê rejoicing.
The heart of the Mistress of Life is gladdened
    for the Enemy of her Lord is overthrown!

You shall see Horus with the tiller-rope,
    and Thoth, with Maat in his arms,
        each god rejoicing.
For they have seen Rê, who comes in triumph
    to sanctify the hearts of the redeemed.

By the osiris, the scribe of offerings for the Lords of Thebes, Ani, vindicated
with them.

41. A Hymn to the Setting Sun
[Ch. XV, Papyrus of Mut-hotepet]

Another saying concerning the mysteries of the underworld: the issuing forth in secret from the realm of the dead to see the Sundisk when he goes to rest in the West; the adoration of him by gods and transfigured spirits in the underworld; and the perfecting of the soul in the presence of Rê—to offer it power through Atum, to exalt it through Osiris, to give it its dignity by means of the Ennead, to guide it through the underworld, to be attentive to its footsteps, and to help it learn to see when it is with the Great God.

As for each spirit which he has created, it shall go forth into the daylight in any form that it may wish, and it shall be powerful among the gods of the underworld so that they shall recognize it as one of them and so that it may enter in all its power into the secret gateway.

Spoken by Mut-hotepet, vindicated:

> Worship for you, Rê-Atum,
> > in your movements, beautiful and glorious,
> When you go down, alive, in the sacred precinct of the
> > > western mountain
> > that you might rest in your field which is in Manu,
> > > your goddess of the rushes attending you.

> Praises to you as you go to rest in peace,
> > you are united with the Eye of Atum;
> The holy serpents place their protection about your flesh
> > as you cross the sky, as you touch down on earth.

> You have ferried across the sunbeams
> > and the dwellings of heaven and earth come to you bowing;
> They offer you adoration each day,
> > and the gods of the West rejoice in your perfections;
> Those in the hidden places worship you,
> > those in the Night Bark row you;
> And the Souls of the East sink down at your Majesty's approach:
> > "Welcome, you who come in peace!"

> There is rejoicing for you,
> > O lord of heaven and ruler of the West!

Your mother, Isis, has protected you
    that she may see her son in you
As lord of awe, exalted in majesty,
    when you go to rest, alive, beyond the threshold.
And your father lifts you up,
    Tatenen puts his arms about you,
One become visible, divine in the body of Earth,
    so that you may be watchful, at peace,
        as you rest within the Western Mountain.

You have placed me as one honored before Osiris!
    O come to me, Rê-Atum!
Let me worship you; may you show love for me;
    let me be vindicated by the Ennead.

You are beautiful, O Rê, in your horizon of the West,
    lord of Truth, exalted in awe,
Mighty in the things you do,
    surpassing in your love of those in the underworld.
You illumine the faces of all those over there
    and all who have withdrawn beyond the horizon.
You light the path to Rosetau, gate of the underworld,
    you have opened the way to Shu and Tefnut;
You place the gods on splendid thrones within their temples,
    and they are joyful as his household propers peacefully
        when Rê goes down.

O you gods of the West who worship Rê-Atum,
    and you who offer praise at his approach,
Employ the arrows of the fallen against the serpent-enemy of Rê;
    oppose him who would wreak destruction on Osiris!
The gods of the West rejoice
    as they take the tow-rope of the Night Bark;
For they have come in triumph
    to voice the Truth of the gods
        whose places in the West are hidden.

O Thoth, who vindicated Osiris against his enemies,
    vindicate Mut-hotepet, whose voice is true, against
        her enemies;

Approach the grand tribunal
    which is with Osiris, Lord of life.
Then the great god who is in the sundisk shall approach,
    Horus, Protector of his Father, Wennefer-rê.
And Osiris shall go to rest
    worshiped by the souls Below.

Praise be to you, being come as Atum,
    come into being as maker of the gods!
Praise be to you, being come as bull of bulls,
    holy one within the horizon!
Praise be to you, more effective than the gods,
    who illuminate the underworld with your Eye!
Praise be to you, who voyage on with your transfigured soul,
    the Sailor in his sundisk.

42. Hymn to the Setting Sun
[Ch. XV, Papyrus Dublin 4]

Adoration of Rê-Horakhty in his going to rest in the western horizon of the sky.

Praises to you, Rê, in your going to rest,
    Atum-Horakhty,
Divinity who created himself,
    primeval one, the first who came into being.
Praises to you, who created the gods,
    who raised up the sky that his eyes might travel its circuit;
Who created earth to be the broad hall for his sunbeams,
    allowing each man to consider his neighbor.

The Night Bark is joyful, the Day Bark shouts praise—
    they have crossed Nun for you victorious,
        and your crew is safe;
The Effective One has felled your enemies,
    for you she destroys the footsteps of Apophis—
        and she is beautiful as Rê each day.

Your mother, Nut, embraces you
    as you go down, perfect in your heart;

There is joy in the horizon of the Western Mountain,
  and the illustrious dead are gladdened.
You shine forth there for the great god,
  Osiris, ruler of eternity.

And the earth-beings in their caverns—
  their arms are raised in adoration of your Person;
And they offer you all their petitions
  once you shed light upon them;
And the lords of the underworld, their hearts are pleased,
  for you have made clear the splendor of the West;
Their eyes are opened wide to look at you,
  and their hearts rejoice when they see you.

May you hear the prayers of those in the grave—
  remove their suffering, drive off their sadnesses!
And may you offer breath of life to their noses
   that they may take the foremost places in your bark
    in the horizon of the Western Mountain.
You are beautiful, O Rê, each day;
  and may your mother, Sky, embrace you.
   The osiris NN, vindicated.

43. Introductory Hymn to Osiris Wennefer
[Ch. XV, Papyrus of Ani]

Praise of Osiris, Wennefer,
  the great god, chief over Abydos,
King of eternity and lord of forever,
  attaining millions of years as his duration;
First son of the womb of Nut,
  whom Geb begat, the heir;
Lord of the double crown, ennobled by the White Crown,
  sovereign of gods and men.
He has received the crook and flail
  and the scepter of his fathers.

Glad is your heart, in the holy Western ground—
  your son, Horus, is established on your throne,

While you shine forth as Lord of Busiris,
 as the ruler who is in Abydos.
For you the Two Lands flourish in vindication
 in the presence of the Lord of All.

He has ushered in the one who has not come to be
 in his Name of Earth-is-Drawn-to-Him;
He has swept the Two Lands clean once more
 in this his Name of Sokar, he who cleanses;
Mighty and magnificent, inspiring awe,
 in this his Name, Osiris, Mighty One.
And he exists at the endpoints of eternity
 in his Name of Wennefer, He who is Perfection.

Praises to you, king of kings
 and lord of lords, ruler of rulers,
Who took the Two Lands for his own in the womb of Nut
 and ruled the regions of the dead;
With fine-gold limbs, a head of lapis lazuli,
 turquoise upon his arms—the pillar of millions—
Broad-chested, with a handsome face;
 now he is in the sacred kingdom of Ta-djeser.

Let me be glorious in the sky, mighty on earth,
 and vindicated in the world below,
Traveling downstream to Busiris as a living Ba,
 moving upstream to Abydos as a heron,
Coming and going without hindrance
 through any gateway of the underworld.
Let me be given bread in the house,
 water and offerings in Heliopolis,
A burial enduring in the Field of Reeds,
 with emmer and barley there.
 For the soul of the osiris, the scribe Ani.

44. Litany to Osiris
[Ch. XV, Papyrus of Ani]

Worship of Osiris, the Lord of Forever:

Wennefer, Horakhty,
 with myriad modes of being, numberless forms,

Ptah-Sokar, Atum in Heliopolis,
>   Lord of the Shrine, who merged with the Temple of Ptah—
These are the gods who govern the underworld;
>   they protect you when you go to rest in Naunet.

Isis wraps you in her peace,
>   the adversary is driven from your path.
You have turned your face toward the West
>   that you may brighten the Two Lands with fine gold!
The sleepers stand to look at you
>   that they may breathe the air, seeing your face;
Just as the Sundisk rising from his horizon,
>   their hearts are pleased with what you have created.
>   For it is you who are eternal and everlasting.

Praise be to you!
>   say the stars in Heliopolis, the Sunfolk in ancient Babylon.
>   You are Wenti, diviner than the gods,
>   the hidden one in Heliopolis.
Praise be to you!
>   say ancient deities of Iwn-des. You are the Great Horakhty,
>   wide-striding when he crosses heaven—
>   You are indeed Horakhty!
Praise be to you!
>   You are the Soul of eternity, the Ram who dwells in Busiris,
>   Wennefer, son of Nut—
>   Lord of the realm of the dead!
Praise be to you,
>   in your rule of Busiris, the Great Crown firm on your head;
>   you are the only one who is his own protection
>   as you go to rest in Busiris.
Praise be to you,
>   lord of the pomegranate nome, one who places Sokar
>   on his sledge,
>   drives off the rebel who does evil,
>   and puts the Eye to rest where it belongs.
Praise be to you,
>   strong in your power, great and mighty,
>   foremost in Naref, master of time and eternity;
>   it is you who are lord of Herakleopolis.

Praise be to you,
    at rest in Truth, it is you who are lord of Abydos,
        who has joined the Sacred Land with your body:
            you are the one who hates falsehood.
Praise be to you,
    in the midst of your sacred bark, you fetch Hapy from
        his cavern,
        one on whose dead body sunlight shines:
            he is the one in Hierakonpolis.
Praise be to you,
    creator of gods, King of Upper and Lower Egypt, Osiris,
        vindicated,
        who founded the Two Lands with his mighty acts:
            this is he, lord of the Two Banks!

May you make me a path
    that I may pass on in peace.
I am one who is straightforward and true.
    I did not speak falsehood knowingly,
        nor did I do an evil thing twice.

VI

Amarna: The Heretical Interlude
of Aton

King Akhenaton of Dynasty 18 (1350–1334 B.C.E.) was the first known monotheist in history. He was a visionary who abolished the traditional polytheism of Egypt and substituted for it his understanding of the creator and sun-god, whom he called Aton. Akhenaton left Thebes to build and live in a new city, today called el-Amarna, where he could worship his god without the trappings or priesthoods of the other gods.

Aton was a benevolent and caring deity, not only the creator of the cosmos but also the nurturer of all creatures. His glory shone forth in the sun, whose light and warmth made life possible. There are several hymns to Aton in the tombs of the courtiers of Akhenaton at Amarna; the finest of them, from the tomb of Aye, is given here.

45. Akhenaton's Hymn to Aton
[Tomb of Aye]

In Praise of the living Horakhty who rejoices in the Horizon in his Name of the divine Light which is in the Sundisk, living eternally and forever, the living Aton, Great One who is in the Festival, Lord of all the sundisk circles, Lord of Heaven, Lord of Earth, Living on Maat, Lord of the Two Lands, Nefer-kheper-rê Wa-en-rê, Son of the Sun, Who lives on Maat, Lord of Appearances, Akhenaton, One Great in his Time; and the Great Royal Wife, whom he loves, Mistress of the Two Lands, Nefer-neferu-aten Nefertiti, living, healthy, flourishing forever and eternity. He says:

i

May you always appear thus gloriously in the horizon of the sky,
    O living Aton, origin of life!
Arisen from the eastern horizon,
    you have filled all earth with your splendor;
You are beautiful, great, dazzling, exalted above each land,
    yet your rays encompass the lands
        to the limits of all which you have created;
There in the Sun, you reach to their boundaries,
    making them bow to your Son, whom you love;
And though you are far, your rays are over the earth,
    and you are in the faces of those who watch your
        jouneying.

ii

You go to rest in the western horizon,
    and earth is in a darkness like death,
With the sleepers in bedchambers, heads covered—
    the eye cannot discern its companion;
All their goods might be carried off—
    though they are near—without their knowing.
Every lion comes forth from his doorway,
    insects and snakes bite and sting;
Darkness shrouds, earth is silent—
    he who created them is at rest in his tomb.

iii

Dawn rises shining on the horizon,
    gleams from the sundisk as day.
You scatter the darkness, bestow your sunbeams,
    and the Two Lands offer thanksgiving.
The Sunfolk awaken and stand on their feet,
    for you have raised them up;
Their bodies are bathed, they put on their clothing,
    their arms raised in praise at your appearing.
Throughout the land
    they take up their work.

iv

The herds are at peace in their meadows,
    trees and the vegetation grow green,
Birds fly from their nests,
    their wings spread wide in praise of your Person;
All the small beasts leap about on their feet,
    and all who fly up or settle to rest
        live because you have shone upon them.
Ships go downstream or upstream as well,
    each path lies open because of your presence;
The fish in the River dart about in your sight,
    and your beams are deep in the Great Green Sea.

v

It is you who create the seed in women,
    shape the fluids into human beings,
Make the son alive in the womb of his mother,
    soothe him, ending his tears,
Nurturer from the womb to those given breath
    to bring into life all that he has created.
He descends from the womb to breathe
    on the day of his birth,
And you open his mouth, determine his nature,
    and minister to his needs.

vi

The fledgling in the egg speaks in the shell,
    so you give him breath within it to succor him;
And you have given to him his allotted time
    so that he might break out from the egg
To come forth peeping at that time
    and move about upon his own two feet
        when he emerges from it.

vii

How various are the things you have created,
    and they are all mysterious to the sight!
O sole God, without another of your kind,

you created the world according to your desire,
      while you were alone,
With mankind and cattle and every sort of small beast,
      all those upon land, those who go upon feet,
Those who are on high soaring upon their wings,
      the foreign lands of Khor and Kush,
            and all that belongs to Egypt.

viii

You give each person his place in life,
      and you provide for his needs;
Each one has his sustenance,
      and his lifetime is reckoned for him.
Tongues are separated by words,
      the natures of persons as well;
And their skins are made different
      so you can distinguish the peoples.

ix

You create Hapy, the Nile, in the Underworld
      to bring him, at your desire, to nourish the people,
Just as you create them for yourself,
      Lord of them all, who is weary for them,
O Lord of all earth, who shines for them,
      O Aton of day, awesome in majesty.
All the foreign lands are far away,
      yet you make their lives possible,
For you have placed a Hapy in the sky
      that he might come down upon them—
Making waves upon the mountains like those of the Great
      Green Sea
      to water the fields in their villages.

x

How well ordered it is, your governing,
      O Lord of Eternity, Hapy in heaven!
You belong to the foreign peoples,
      to the small beasts of each land who go upon feet.
And Hapy comes from Below to beloved Egypt as well,

while your rays are nursing each meadow.
You shine, and they live,
    they grow strong for you;
You fashion the seasons to make all your creation flourish—
    the winter for cooling
        and the heat which ripens;
And you have made the sky far off
    in order to shine down from it,
        to watch over all you have created.

xi

You are one alone,
    shining forth in your visible Form as the living Aton,
Glorious, giving light,
    far-off yet approaching nearby.
You create the numberless visible forms from yourself—
    you who are one alone—
Cities, towns, fields, the road, the River;
    and each eye looks to you as its shining example:
You are in the sun-disk of day,
    overseer of wherever you go and whatever shall be;
For you fashion their sight so that you may be complete—
    [as they] celebrate with one [voice] your creation.

xii

And you are in my heart;
    there is no other who knows you
Except for your son, Akhenaton,
    Nefer-kheper-rê Wa-en-rê.
Let him be wise with your counsel, your strength,
    that the world may approach your condition
        just as when you created it.
You have risen, and they are alive;
    you go to rest, and they die.
For you are the measure of Time itself,
    one lives by means of you.
Eyes shall be filled with beauty until your setting;
    all labor is set aside when you go to rest in the West.
Then rise! Let [the creatures of earth] thrive for the king!

And let me hasten on with every footstep
[as I have] since you founded the world.
And raise them up for your son
who came forth from your very body.

The King of Upper and Lower Egypt, who lives on Truth, Lord of the Two Lands, Nefer-Kheper-Rê Wa-en-rê, son of the Sun, who lives on Truth, Lord of Appearances, Akhenaton, one exalted in his own lifetime; and the Great Royal Wife, whom he loves, Nefer-neferu-aton Nefertiti, who lives and flourishes for eternity and everlasting.

VII

Hymns and Prayers to Other Deities
The Riches of Polytheism

Egypt was rich in gods. At the center of consciousness was the Heliopolitan Ennead, with special prominence given to Rê and Osiris and their stories. But there were many others, almost as prominent. Hathor was a great goddess with many aspects, sometimes functioning as the mother of Horus, sometimes as a funerary deity, and sometimes as the goddess of love and intoxication. Thoth was the god of wisdom, scrivener to the gods, preserver of the holy scriptures, and protector of scribes. Ptah was the creator god, according to the theology of Memphis (rather than Heliopolis), but he was also the god of craftsmen and artisans. Hapy was the god of the Nile River in flood, the energy that brought return of the waters each year, unseen and without temples. Maat is a case of personification: she emerged from the head of Rê as a goddess representing the fundamental Egyptian values of Truth, Justice, and Order.

46. Hymn and Prayer to Ptah
[Papyrus Harris I]

Spoken by the King, Usermaatrê Meramun, the great god under his Father, this splendid god, great Ptah, South of his Wall, lord of the life of the lands, Tatenen, father of the gods, exalted in the double plume, with sharp horns, the Handsome of Face upon the Great Throne:

The Hymn

Greetings to you, exalted ancient one,
    O Tatenen, father of the gods,
Eldest god of the primeval time,
    who shaped mankind and formed the gods;
Who began Becoming as the first primeval god—
    every event that occurred came after him.
Who created the sky according to what his heart imagined
    and raised it up like one lifts up a feather;
Who founded the world as his own creation,
    circled it about with Ocean and the Great Green Sea;
Who made the underworld, provided for the dead,
    allowing Rê to sail across below to comfort them
        as Ruler of Eternity, Lord of Forever.

Lord of life, who causes throats to breathe,
    who offers air to every nostril,
        who lets all people live through his provisions.
Time, fate, and fortune are under his dominion—
    we live by that which issues from his mouth.
Who created the offerings for all the gods
    when he embodied himself as Nun, the primal waters.
Lord of eternity—the everlasting is under his care—
    he breathes out life for everyone,
And guides the king to his great Throne
    in his Name of King of the Two Lands.

The Prayer

I am your son, whom you installed as king
    on the throne of my father, peacefully;
And I am upon your waters,
    your good counsel is with me.
May you double good things for me
    while I am upon earth.
May you draw me toward rest at your side in the West of heaven
    just as you do for all the hidden gods of the otherworld—
A friend of your Enneads in your secret precinct
    like Apis, your splendid Soul, who is at your side.

    the bread, incense, beer, shedeh, and wine.
Let me live again within the Sacred Realm;
    and let me see you daily as your two Enneads do.
But while I am Ruler upon earth as lord of the Beloved Land,
    let me not keep my heart from zealousness for you—
Seeking out all that is useful for your splendid dwelling,
    governing well before you in your City of the Wall.

[*There follows a description of the temple Ramesses III will build.*]

47. Prayer to Ptah, Sakhmet, Ptah-Sokar, and Osiris
[Statue of Horemheb in New York]

A gift of the living king to Ptah South of his Wall, Sakhmet, beloved of Ptah, Ptah-Sokar, lord of Shetyt, and Osiris, lord of Rosetau:

May you all allow my Soul to come forth in the day
    to see the Sundisk;
May you listen to me praying every day
    like the transfigured spirits whom you made so glorious;
And may you have me follow you both day and night
    as one of those you honor,
Because I am one who has been true to God
    since first I was on earth.
Let me satisfy Truth, truly, every day,
    for I have turned my back on evil in his presence,
        nor has there been occasion [for it] since my birth.

For surely I am one who is benevolent under God,
    wise and contented, who listens to the truth.
Let me be among the crew in the bark of Osiris
    celebrating in the district of Peqer.

For the Spirit of the hereditary prince, Sole Friend, royal deputy for the Two Lands, royal scribe, Horemheb, vindicated.

48. Hymn to Thoth
[Statue of Horemheb in New York]

Worship of Thoth, son of Rē, beautiful emergent Moon, lord of appearances, who illumines the gods, by the hereditary prince, mayor, vizier, fanbearer on the king's right hand, commander in chief of the armies, royal scribe, Horemheb, vindicated. He says:

> Praises to you, O moon, Djehuty,
>> strong bull of Hermopolis, dwelling in its sacred precinct,
> One who clears the way for the gods, knows the religious mysteries,
>> writes down the statements of the gods;
> Who distinguishes one report from another like it
>> and evaluates each person;
> Skilled to guide the Bark of Millions of Years;
>> courier for the Sunfolk,
> Who knows a man by his speech
>> and measures the deed against the doer.
>
> Who attends on Rē, ascends to the presence of the sole Lord
>> to inform him of all that has happened—
> Each dawn he gives an accounting in the sky;
>> and he does not neglect the events of yesterday.
>
> Who keeps the Night Bark healthy
>> and makes the Day Bark peaceful,
> His arms unhindered in the prow of the Night Bark,
>> clear-seeing when he has taken the rope of the Day Bark,
> Rejoicing in the joy of the Night Bark
>> during the celebration when it crosses the sky.
>
> Who overthrows the Rebel-Serpent
>> and calculates the landing on the Western horizon,
> While the Ennead in the Night Bark offers praise to Thoth,
>> saying to him,
> 'Hail! Hail! O you whom Rē favors
>> as you compose the paeans to the gods."
> They re-echo what your spirit wishes
>> as you open a path to the destination of the Bark.
> May you sacrifice that Rebel-Serpent, cut his head off,

annihilate his soul, and throw his body on the fire,
        for you are the god who slaughters him.

There is nothing done without your knowing
        as the Exalted One, son of the Great Goddess,
                who came forth from her flesh;
Protector of Horakhty, with entrée to the lore of Heliopolis,
        who created the sphere of the gods,
Who knows the sacred Mysteries,
        interpreter of their words.

Let us offer praise to Thoth,
        the plumbline which is true in the center of the balance,
Who drives off evil,
        receives the one who does not lean toward crime,
Vizier who judges words, who quiets uproars into peace,
        scribe of records who protects the scrolls,
Who punishes the guilty, accepts the one in chains,
        healthy of arm, wisest of the Ennead,
Who brings back all forgotten things,
        helpful to one who has gone astray,
Who recalls the fleeting moment,
        who reports on each hour of the darkness;
Whose words will last forever—
        who has entrée to the Underworld,
Knowing all those there,
        and who records them, each according to his name.

49. Prayer to Thoth
[Statue of Horemheb in New York]

An offering of the king to Thoth, lord of the sacred writings, lord of Hermopolis, who determines Truth, and who ferries Rê in the Night Bark. May you cause that the following words be accurate:

I am one forthright with the courtiers:
        each problem is reported to me,
                and my tongue is skilled enough to set it right.

I am one who upholds the laws of the King,
>who gives instructions to the courtiers;
>>wise in my speech, there is nothing of which I am ignorant.

I am one who gives guidance to all,
>who helps each man to know his way,
>>and I do not forget what is put in my charge.

I am one who advises the Lord of the Two Lands,
>who speaks of things neglected,
>>who does not ignore what my Lord has said.

I am one who reports to the Council;
>>and I do not forget the counsels of his Majesty.
>>For the Spirit of the hereditary prince Horemheb,
>>>vindicated.

50. Hymn to Thoth and Maat
[British Museum Stele 551]

Praises to you, Djehuty, Lord of Hermopolis,
>who came to be of himself, not being born;

Sole god, who governs the underworld,
>who gives instruction to the Westerners—

Those who are in the retinue of Rê—
>and who distinguishes among the tongues of all the lands.

May you allow Horemheb, the royal scribe, to flourish at his
>>Sovereign's side
>just as you are beside the Lord of All,
>>just as you nurtured him when he came forth from
>>>the womb.

And praise to Maat, our Lady of the Northwind,
>who opens the nostrils of the living
>>and who gives air to the One in the midst of his bark.

Allow Prince Horemheb to breathe the breezes born of heaven
>just as the Lady of Punt breathes her aromas from the Lake
>>of Myrrh.

May you allow my entry and departure from the Field of Reeds,
>and let me be provided there from the Field of Offerings,

and receive the daily gifts from the altars of the Lords
  of Heliopolis;
And let my heart be in the water-crossing from the Necropolis
  to the pure islands of the Field of Reeds.
May you open wide to me the blessed path
  and spread my road before me,
    and may you place me in the retinue of Sokar
      before the gates of the Beyond.

For the Spirit of the hereditary prince, Sole Friend, Commander in Chief
of the Armies, rejoicing under Osiris, Horemheb, vindicated, possessor of
blessedness.

51. Khety's Hymn to the Nile

The Praising of Hapy

i

Praises to you, Hapy,
  one who springs from the earth, come to save Egypt;
With hidden features, a darkness by day,
  to whom his followers give praise;
Who waters the countryside created by Rê
  to give life to each kind of small creature;
Who satisfies the upland, the pathway, the water's edge—
  and he is the very dew, as it falls from heaven;
Beloved of Geb, the one who guides Nepri,
  who makes the crafts of Ptah flourish.

ii

Lord of the fish, who makes wildfowl fly south—
  and no birds fall by command of the winds—
Who creates barley, brings emmer to be,
  richly provisions the temples.
But let him be sluggish, then noses stop up,
  then every face is poverty-stricken;
If one destroys the offering-cakes of the gods,
  then millions are perished from among mankind.

iii

Who creates the rapacious man to trouble the land—
    great men and small are found wandering.
But people mingle together when he draws near,
    when Khnum fashions him on his potter's wheel.
Let him rise, then earth is joyful,
    then every belly rejoices;
Backbones have taken to laughter,
    each tooth is bared.

iv

Who brings food and abundant provisions,
    who himself creates all his good things;
Majestic, fragrant of aromas,
    one is at peace when he comes.
Who brings pastures to be for the cattle
    and provides the sacrifices for each god.
He is in the underworld, yet heaven and earth are under his rule,
    and he takes the Two Lands for his own,
Filling the storehouses, enlarging the granaries,
    providing goods for the poor.

v

Who makes each desirable tree flourish
    so that one shall never lack for it;
Who makes shipping possible by means of his force
    so the ship will not sink like a stone.
Bluffs are seized in his surging,
    yet he cannot be seen.
Who works yet he cannot be governed,
    he is well-versed in the Mysteries.
One cannot know the place where he is
    nor spy his source from the writings.

vi

Floodwaters cut through the villages—there is no stopping them—
    they wander about, and no guiding them;
Troops of the young accompany him,

and they greet him with honors like a king;
Whose ways are enduring, who comes in his season,
    who fills both Lower and Upper Egypt.
Every eye is moistened through him
    who provides an excess of his good things.

vii

Poised at the entrance, he comes forth gladly,
    and every heart rejoices;
Who conceived Sobek, child of the floodwaters,
    and holy the Ennead, which is from him.
Who spits out the fields, sails over his marshland,
    gives provisions to all mankind;
Makes one man powerful to weaken another—
    and there is no contending against him—
He makes his own peace, will not be threatened,
    lets no boundaries be set for him.

viii

Who illumines those who go forth in darkness
    with the tallow of cattle;
All that has come to be is through his strength,
    no district of the living is ignorant of him.
Who clothes mankind with flax, which he originated,
    letting the weaver-god get to his work;
Who provides the god of orchards with his gums
    so that Ptah can fasten things with his glues.
Who provides [. . . . .] for Khepri—
    all workers come into being through him;
All writings belong to the words of God
    through his providing papyrus.

ix

Who enters the underworld, emerges again,
    revealer, who comes forth with secrets.
But should he lie heavy, his subjects are few—
    the food supply of that year is destroyed.
Then one may see Thebans like women—
    each man destroys his implements;

There is no thread for products,
    there is no cloth for clothing,
There is no adorning the children of the rich,
    no cosmetics for their faces;
The trees have been ruined for lack of him—
    there is no perfuming anyone.

x

Who plants Justice firm in the hearts of mankind
    when they would speak lies of the helpless among them;
Who mingles together with the Great Green Sea
    but does not try to control its waters;
Who gives praise to all the gods,
    never letting a bird fall to his desert.
There is no crossing his palm with gold,
    no man gets drunk upon silver,
One cannot eat lapis lazuli—
    food comes before prosperity.

xi

They begin songs to the harp for him,
    chantresses clap their hands,
Troops of the young shout for him,
    a body of retainers is prepared for him—
And he returns bearing riches, decorates this land,
    makes the features and flesh of mankind flourish,
Nourishes the thoughts of women with child,
    desiring multitudes of all creatures.

xii

He rises among hungry citizens,
    and they are satisfied with his fruits of the fields—
Fresh greens for the mouth, lotuses for the nose—
    and all good things spill over the land.
Each plant has its offspring—
    all have forgotten to eat!
Good is strewn through the parishes;
    this entire land is dancing!

xiii

Hapy surges, and offering is made to him,
  for him cattle are slaughtered;
For him great feasts are held,
  for him fowl are fattened,
For him lions are captured out in the desert,
  for him beautiful things are provided.
And they make offering to each god
  just like what has been done for Hapy—
Finest incense, short- and long-horned cattle, and birds for
      burnt offering—
    and Hapy, down in his secret cavern, is powerful.
Yet his name cannot be known in the underworld,
  nor can the very gods reveal it.

xiv

All mankind extols the Nine Great Gods,
  who stand in awe of that Majesty
Which aids his divine son, Lord of All,
  to make green the Two Banks of the Nile.
O thrive, then you will come! Thrive, then you will come!
  O Hapy, thrive, then you will come!
Come back to Egypt, O you who bring satisfaction and peace,
  making green the Two Banks of the Nile.
Give life to mankind and the creatures
  through your gifts from the countryside!
O thrive, then you will come! Thrive, then you will come!
  O Hapy, thrive, then you will come!

52. Ramesside Hymn to the Nile
[Ostracon Deir el-Medineh 1675]

i

. . . .
    . . . .
. . . in praise of Hapy
    to exalt all his perfections.

Father of . . . .
          . . . . [as] he comes in his season;
And every heart rejoices
          at this compensation for his years of hesitation.
. . . .
          . . . . his good things.

ii

He has come forth
          from his mysterious cavern;
And furious, he rages on his winding way . . . . . .
          coming to rest upon the highest ground—
Wave fights riverbank,
          and earth is in chaos, like Nun.
. . . . dread;
          for he is like a lion who has sprung forth!
Egypt is awakened,
          its lethargy is gone!
All the creatures celebrate
          when he greens the Two Banks of the Nile,
When he pours forth abundance
          among the old and the young alike.

iii

Lovely the lotus, whose blossoms dot the flood
          that they may tell the happiness to come;
Each creeping thing
          rejoices in its dwelling;
Insects call on Hapy while they dance on air
          or buzz upon the banks—
They announce the birth of children,
          and the frog booms for happiness.
Faces are joyful
          and take to cheering.

iv

To the ends of the land it grows green,
          there is so much food one wearies to see it;
Good things are strewn in the gateways

and abundance surfeits the stomach.
Teeth are sweet with dates
    and laughter comes forth;
The back turns away from complaining
    and unbounded happiness dispels tribulation.

                              v

All hearts fashion praise,
    they know not dejection.
There is joy in discovering beauty,
    new growth covers the land he has moistened.
The young plants are bowed down
    bearing their fruit,
The reeds and rushes are splendid
    and the sa'amu-plants are gleaming;
Blossoms are at their best
    and all the trees are flourishing;
The staff-of-life plants have offered their fruit
    and cannot hide their fragrance.

                              vi

Ears breathe in beckonings,
    hearts receive messages.
The small do not curse the distinguished,
    the low show respect for the great;
The young offer praise to their Lord,
    and the powerful chasten the boastful.
The governance of the Residence
    is like what had been before in the palace—
        with Maat in the mouths of the magistrates.
The great winejars are pregnant with wine,
    and teeth are joined to fine ale;
The eyes of the curious gaze about,
    and limbs are clothed in red linen.

                              vii

The temples are splendid with services,
    offerings take place at the altars;
Double doors swing wide for the Lords of Eternity

and the falcon-gods are content.
The torches flare on the breeze,
    and the homes of the gods are brightened.
. . . .
    . . . . the blessed dead.

viii

[The Book?] of the Audience Chamber is brought to light,
    and the Book of Governing has been found.
Crocodiles rage, plunging about to their heart's desire,
    and the waters are fresh with their voices;
The fish are swollen with roe
    which are set free in the flood.

ix

Wildfowl halt on the edge of the Faiyum lakes
    or havens on the earth-mounds of the South;
The Delta-Northland will become their nesting-place;
    the feathers of the ro-geese gleam.
Fowlers snare,
    their arrows catch good things.

x

Papyrus plants grow green bearing their seeds,
    the transport ships are weighed down with their stalks.
Bulls bellow when they see their thickets,
    young animals nurse at their mothers.
All plots of ground give birth to food,
    and jars are filled with cream.
The small beasts of the valley scurry, chattering,
    their fur is rich and smooth and needs no grooming;
The ostrich leaps up when he spies his vine-plants,
    his offspring are sated and sleepy.

xi

The poor are like the highest of the land,
    and the great are like the humble;
The man of low degree attains to power

so that he brings forth barley;
Emmer is created for him,
    and the hunter [hunts for him].
Each lock of hair drips with sweet-oil,
    and the bees are making honey.

xii

Come, O god, ...
    Hapy, do not be slow!
And do not be oppressive, lessening what we have,
    for you might wrong [the innocent] . . . . . .
May you yourself [give breath] to his nose when you come;
    O Hapy, do not sink into the ground;
There are no . . . .
    . . . . his prayers.
Your perfection is here before us
    that we may turn back to your keeping;
        and the gods are near.

53. Hymn to Maat
[Temple of Amun at el-Hibis]

A recitation by the King, Lord of the Two Lands, son of Rê, who lives forever: Maat gives praise to her fathers, Amun-Rê and Ptah.

Praise to you, Maat, daughter of Rê,
    consort of god, whom Ptah loves,
The one who adorns the breast of Thoth, who fashioned
        her own nature,
    foremost of the Souls of Heliopolis;
Who pacified the two falcon gods through her good will,
    filled the Per-wer shrine with life and dominion;
Skilled one who brought forth the gods from herself
    and brought low the heads of the enemies;
Who herself provides for the House of the All-Lord,
    brings daily offerings for those who are on duty.
Magnificent her throne before the judges—
    and she consumes the enemies of Atum.

She is just,
>and there is no injustice in the Son of Rê, who lives forever.
Shu commingling with Thoth—
>his body is filled, through her, with mankind
>>which he offers to Amun-Rê, Ptah, and Amun of Hibis.
And the Great Ennead is powerful
>in the House of the Prince in Heliopolis.

Rise splendidly, O Rê,
>how beautiful you are because of Maat!
As Maat shines splendid from the heart of Rê,
>so are you splendid, O King, Son of Rê, who lives forever;
You too are beautiful because of Maat—
>see her who comes to the Son of Rê, who lives forever!

O Maat, build your throne in the head, in the mouth,
>of the King, Son of Rê, who lives forever!
May you make heaven and earth rejoice in Rê his father
>from whom I, the King, have come forth.
May you rise splendid from him on this beautiful day
>in this your divine Name of Khayt—
>>She who appears in beauty.
And may your beautiful face give peace
>to this good god, lord of the Two Lands, Darius,
>>son of the Sun and living forever.

54. Prayer to Hathor as Goddess of Love
[Papyrus Chester Beatty I]

Let me worship the Golden One to honor her Majesty
>and exalt the Lady of Heaven;
Let me give adoration to Hathor
>and songs of joy to my heavenly Mistress!
I beg her to hear my petitions
>that she send me my mistress now!

And she came herself to see me!
>What a great thing that was when it happened!

I rejoiced, I was glad, I was exalted,
     from the moment they said, "Oh, look at her!
"See, here she comes!"—and the young men bowing
     through their enormous passion for her.

Let me consecrate breath to my Goddess
     that she give me my Love as a gift!
It is four days now I have prayed in her name;
     let her be with me today!

VIII

The Nature of the Beyond
The Prayers of Pahery

Pahery lived during earlier Dynasty 18 and was mayor of el-Kab and Esna. The walls of his tomb at el-Kab offer the most extensive characterization of the afterlife that survives from ancient Egypt. From his prayers and descriptions we can see the function of his tomb and the necessity of regular offerings to sustain his soul. We also follow his vision of what life with Osiris would be like and of the possibilities for moving back and forth between this world (as an invisible spirit) and the next (as one of the glorious redeemed). It is also interesting to note the presence in Pahery's prayers of the concept of "the god within" the living human breast.

55. The Prayers of Pahery

i

Prayer to the Gods for Offerings

An offering which the king makes:— to Amun,
    Lord of the Thrones of the Two Lands,
King of eternity, lord of forever,
    divine Ruler, lord of the high double plume,
Sole one beforetimes, greatest of Ancients of primeval days,
    without equal, creator of men and gods,
Living flame which rose out of chaos
    in order to lighten the Sunfolk;

And to Nekhbet, the Shining One,
    Mistress of Heaven, Lady of the Two Lands;
To Osiris, Foremost of Westerners,
    Lord of This, great in Abydos;
To Hathor, mistress of desert borders,
    fearless among the gods;
To Ptah-Sokar, lord of Shetyt;
    to Anubis, lord of Rosetau;
And to the Enneads, the Greater and Lesser:—

May They give a thousand of bread, beer, meat, and fowl,
    a thousand offerings of provisions,
A thousand offerings of every plant
    which flourishes upon earth,
And a thousand of everything good and pure
    which is offered in the presence of the All-Lord.
And may They receive the bread and drink which is before
       the Lord of Eternity
    and the milk which appears upon the offering table,
And the water which gushes forth from Elephantine,
    and the northwind which [blows over the land]—
At the festivals of the Month, the Sixth Day, the Half-Month,
    the Great Procession, the Rising of Sothis,
The feast of jubilation, of Thoth,
    of the First Birth of Osiris, of Isis,
The Procession of Min, the Procession of the Fourth Day,
    the Evening Offering, the Rising of the River,
And the festivals of heaven according to their days
    and according to the daily rituals.

May They provide for you a sacred robe of finest linen
    from those taken from the limbs of the god;
May They anoint you with sacred oil,
    may you drink the water that is left upon the altar,
And may you receive offerings from what is upon it,
    as one honored among the foremost of the blessed.

For the Soul of the Mayor of el-Kab, the scribe Pahery, vindicated,
    filled with devotion to his Lord.

ii
Prayer for Life in the Afterworld

May you come and go, while living,
    with joyful heart by favor of the Lord of gods,
With a fine burial in old age,
    after your length of years has come.
May you take your place in your sarcophagus,
    unite with earth in the Western Land,
Become transformed to a living Spirit
    —powerful over bread, and water, and air—
Which may take shape as phoenix or swallow,
    as falcon or heron, just as you wish.

May you ferry across without hindrance
    and sail upon the waters of the flood.
May your life return once more—
    your spirit never deserting your body again!
May your spirit be holy among the transfigured,
    and may the blessed hold converse with you;
Your likeness is there among them in heaven
    while you are receiving your offerings on earth.

May you have power over water, breathe air,
    drink whatever your heart desires;
May you be given your eyes to see with,
    your ears for hearing whatever is said,
Your mouth for speaking,
    and your feet to walk.
May your arms move for you, and your shoulders,
    your flesh be firm, your muscles thriving;
May you have joy of all your members
    and count your body whole and well.

No evil is accountable to you,
    your heart is with you truly;
Your mind is yours as formerly
    as you go forth to the sky.

May you explore the afterworld
    in whatsoever shape you shall desire.

May they call you every day
    to the Table of Osiris, who was truly good;
And may you enjoy the offerings in His presence
    and the gifts for the Lord of the Sacred Land.

For the Soul of the Mayor of el-Kab, the Mayor of Esna,
    Counter of Grain from Denderah to el-Kab,
The vigilant administrator free of wrongdoing,
    the scribe Pahery, vindicated.

iii
Prayer Describing the Afterlife

May you eat the loaves in the presence of God
    by the Great Staircase of the Lord of the Ennead;
May you turn from there to the place where he is
    in the midst of the high tribunal of judges;
May you move about freely among them,
    a friend to the Followers of Horus.

May you come and go unhindered
    and not be turned back from the doors of the otherworld;
May the gates of heaven be opened to you,
    and the very doorbolts unlock of themselves;
May you enter the Hall of Two Truths
    and the god who is in it honor you.

May you be at ease in the underworld,
    travel freely about in the city of Hapy;
May your heart have joy in your ploughing
    in your plot in the Field of Reeds;
May your portion reach what has been set for you
    and the harvest arrive full of grain;
May the draw-rope be taut in the ferryboat—
    Sail to your heart's desire!

May you go forth from the tomb each dawn
    and find your way back each evening.
May they kindle a taper for you at night

until the sun shines on your breast.
Let them say to you, "Welcome, welcome
    to your house of the ever-living!"

May you gaze upon Rê in the circuit of Heaven
    and glimpse Amun when he shines;
May you be mindful of beauty each day,
    may all that impedes you be driven to earth;
May you spend eternity in gladness of heart
    esteemed by the god who is within you.
—Your heart is with you, it will never abandon you;
    and your provisions endure in their place.

For the soul of the scribe, Pahery, vindicated.

iv
Pahery's Autobiography: His Claim of Rectitude

He says:
I was a nobleman, effective for his lord,
    wise, not negligent.
I proceeded on the path which I sought out
    and came to understand the goal of living.
I reckoned up the farthest limits in those writings
    which dealt with actions of the king;
And all the affairs of the royal palace
    were smooth as Hapy flowing to the Great Green Sea.

My voice was skilled in furthering the interests of my lord,
    concerned as I was with balancing accounts;
I was not neglectful of the payments,
    nor did I profit from the surpluses.
My own heart guided me
    along the path to praises of the king.

My pen made me famous;
    it made my voice heard among the magistrates,
And it enhanced my reputation
    so that I outdistanced noblemen.

[. . . . .] me in the Presence,
    and my good character elevated me—
Summoned as one unbiased and placed in the balance,
    I emerged as one esteemed and trusted, without taint.

I came and went
    with my heart my sole companion.
I did not speak falsely to another person,
    knowing the god who dwells in humankind—
I could perceive Him
    and thus distinguish one path from another.
I acted exactly as commanded,
    did not confuse report with its reporter;
I did not speak the language of the streets
    nor consort with those of little character.

I was one who attained benevolence,
    one praised who came forth favored from the womb.
The mayor of el-Kab, Pahery,
    begotten of the Prince's tutor, the Scribe Itef-reri, vindicated,
        and born to the Mistress of the Estate, Kam, vindicated.

υ
Appeal to the Living

He says:
    Pray listen, all you who have now come to be,
        let me speak to you without equivocation!
    O living ones, you who exist,
        nobles and commons who are upon the earth,
    Servants of god hallowed in their calling,
        each scribe who bears the staff of office,
    The one conversant with god's language,
        each one skilled in dealing with subordinates,
            the speaker distinguished for his readings of the liturgy—
    May you all give praise to Rê, Lord of Eternity,
        and to Nekhbet, the Shining Goddess of el-Kab.
    And all of you passersby, effective in your varied offices,
        may you live to endow your children!

Just so, may you recite the offering prayer
    in the manner found in the writings
And the invocation offering as spoken by those long dead
    just as it came from the mouth of God.
Anyone who shall here bend his arm
    shall grow in the counsels of righteousness;
To act properly according to tradition
    is to bear witness before this gravestone:
Your thousand of bread, your thousand of beer,
    your hundred-thousand of everything good, true, and pure,
For the osiris, mayor of el-Kab, mayor of Esna,
    treasurer on the southward voyage,
        the scribe excellent at reckoning, Pahery, vindicated.

Let me speak to you all,
    help you to understand:
This is a recitation without excesses or exaggerations—
    there is no slander, no disputation in it,
There is no contending with another person,
    no troubling some poor man in his misery.

These are sweet words of consolation!
    The mind cannot be surfeited with hearing them!
The breath of the mouth can never be used up—
    there is no breathlessness, no weariness in this.
Goodness is yours when you perform it
    for [you] discover [that it earns] you favor.

While I was on earth among the living,
    no injustices toward god were counted against me,
        and I became a blessed spirit.
Oh! I have furnished my house in the realm under god,
    and my share is by me in everything.
Yet I shall not fail to answer a prayer—
    a dead man is father to any who aid him;
He does not forget one who pours water to honor him.
    It is good for you to consider this.

Hymns, Prayers, and Praises
to Pharaoh
The Divine King

Whereas the hymns and prayers of the Pyramid Texts were entirely con-
cerned with the dead king undergoing resurrection, the following songs of
praise, hymns, and prayers are directed to the living king. The first several
poems reflect the era of the Middle Kingdom, while the remainder are from
the later New Kingdom, the Ramesside period. In them all, the reader can
taste the flavor of the adulation offered the pharaoh by his subjects. It was
quite appropriate for the king to receive such praise and worship; for he was
a god on earth.

56. Ode to Senusert I
[From *The Tale of Sinuhe*]

He is a god indeed, without an equal,
    no other came to be before him;
A master of wisdom, excellent in counsel,
    brilliant in his use of words.
Going and coming are at his command,
    and it is he subdues the foreign lands.
His father is within the palace;
    so he reports to him what he decides shall happen.

He is powerful too, acting with mighty arm,
    vigorous, there are none like him.

He can be seen as he descends upon the foreigners
    once he has entered battle;
He bends the bow, weakens enemy hands,
    rebels cannot group for opposition.
And he is terrible, smashing foreheads;
    no one can stand in his vicinity.

He is far-striding, shooting fugitives—
    no help is there for one who turns the back to him.
Steadfast at the moment of assault,
    he faces forward, never turns *his* back.
Stouthearted he observes the multitudes,
    allows no stragglers in his neighborhood;
Bold to fall on easterners,
    impatient to despoil the foreigners.

Let him but seize his gear for combat,
    he need not raise his arm a second time to kill;
There are none who can flee his arrow,
    none who can draw his bow.
Foreigners scatter all before him
    as from the angry power of the Mighty Goddess.
Fighting in his absence ends—
    he cannot linger for the residue.

Yet he is kindly, full of sweetness,
    taking charge of the land by his affection;
Citizens love him more than their own selves,
    they rejoice in him more than their own local gods.
Husbands and wives pass by exulting in him
    because he is king;
He took possession while still in the womb,
    his face on the kingship since the day he was born.

He ensures that offspring are many about him;
    yet he is one alone, given of God.
This land rejoices in his dominion—
    he is the one to broaden its borders.
He shall seize for his own the lands of the south,
    he need never think twice about the lands of the north.

He was born to strike down Asiatics
and to trample the desert wanderers into dust.

57. Prayer of the Princesses for Clemency
[From *The Tale of Sinuhe*]

Your lot is more than splendid, O King,
who wear the emblems of the Queen of Heaven;
The Golden Goddess offers life unto your nostrils;
and the Lady of the Stars protects you;
The White-Crown Goddess travels north, the Red goes south,
joining together with the utterance of your Majesty;
Wadjet is placed upon your brow.
You have saved the poor from misery;
you have gladdened Rê, Lord of the Two Lands—
praises to you, and to the Mistress of the World as well!

Slacken your bow, put down your arrow,
give breath to one who suffocates!
Give us this lovely gift—
this sheikh, Sa-mehyt, Son of the Northwind,
a bowman born in our beloved land.
He took to flight for fear of you,
he fled the land in terror of you.
But yet, no face should ever blanch at seeing yours,
no eye should fear to gaze upon you.

58. Songs to Senusert III
[Papyrus Kahun LV.1]

For the Horus, Netcherkheperu, the Two Ladies, Netchermesut, the
Golden Horus, Kheper, King of Upper and Lower Egypt, Khakaurê, son of
Rê, Senusert—who takes the Two Lands in triumph:

i. The King as Conquering Hero

Greetings to you, Khakaurê,
our Horus who embodies the divine,

Protects the land, widens its borders,
    and conquers foreign countries by power of his crown,
Uniting the Two Lands through his mighty arm,
    [subduing] the foreign lands by his own hand;
Who can slaughter bowmen without striking a blow
    and shoot an arrow without drawing the bowstring;
Who instills the tribesmen in their lands with terror
    and slays the Nine Peoples by means of fear;
Whose slaughters cause the deaths of thousands
    among those tribes who try to cross his borders,
Shooting arrows like Sakhmet,
    overthrowing thousands who ignore his might—
The tongue of his Majesty overawes Nubia,
    his very words scatter the Asiatics.

Sole Horus, youth divine,
    who [keeps watch] over his borders,
Who does not allow his servants to weary
    but lets the people rest till dawn
While his young folk take their sleep—
    his heart is their protector;
His decrees have marked out his boundaries,
    his word has gathered the Two Banks together.

ii. A Litany of Rejoicing

How happy are the gods,
    for you have maintained their offerings!
How happy are your children,
    for you have established their domain!
How happy are your fathers who were before,
    for you have increased their portion!
How happy are Egyptians in your strength,
    for you have protected the ancient heritage!
How happy is mankind under your governing,
    for your mighty power has received their lives unto itself!
How happy are the Two Banks in awe of you,
    for you have increased their possessions!

How happy are your young men of the army,
>   for you have allowed them to prosper!
How happy are the old and venerable,
>   for you have caused them to feel young again!
How happy are the Two Lands in your strength,
>   for you have protected their citadels!

Refrain: O Horus who broadens his borders, may you go on forever.

iii. The Greatness of the King

How great is the Lord of his city!
>   He is exalted a thousand times over; other persons are small.
How great is the Lord of his city!
>   He is a dike which holds back the River, restraining its flood
>   of water.
How great is the Lord of his city!
>   He is a cool room which lets each man sleep until dawn.
How great is the Lord of his city!
>   He is a rampart with walls of copper from Sinai.
How great is the Lord of his city!
>   He is a refuge which does not lack his helping hand.
How great is the Lord of his city!
>   He is a fort which rescues the fearful man from his enemy.
How great is the Lord of his city!
>   He is a sunshade to help keep cool in summer.
How great is the Lord of his city!
>   He is a warm dry nook in winter.
How great is the Lord of his city!
>   He is the mountain which blocks the storm in a time of
>   raging sky.
How great is the Lord of his city!
>   He is Sakhmet against the enemies who test his borders.

iv. His Protecting Power

He came to us to seize the Southland,
>   and the Double Crown was firm on his head.

He came, he united the Two Lands,
  he mingled the Sedge and the Bee.
He came, he ruled the Egyptians,
  he placed the desert under his control.
He came, he protected the Two Lands,
  he pacified the Two Banks.
He came, he nourished the Egyptians,
  he dispelled their troubles.
He came, he saved the nobles,
  he let the throats of the commoners breathe.
He came, he trampled the foreigners,
  he struck down the tribes who did not fear him.
He came, he descended to his frontiers,
  he rescued those who had been injured.
He came, his arms [received] the veneration
  for what his power had brought to us.
He came, [he helped us raise] our children,
  we have buried our elders [with his blessing].

59. To Pharaoh Coming to Thebes for His Jubilee
[Ostracon Wilson 100]

Praises to you, O divine one who comes to Thebes
  asking for strength [from] her.
The districts celebrate with cries of satisfaction—
  our prayers are heard by Rê, the One who Illumines;
The House of the Scepter is exalted, her fame far-reaching,
  and the son of Rê rejoices.
The great memorial stelae reach to the sky
  because of this epiphany of him who is divine overlord;
The Eight Great Gods are bowed, their arms bent in homage,
  their mouths directed downward—
    all their strength is for the Flourishing One.

Enter, that you may be renewed within,
  that you may step forth again more than perfect.
Praises are chanted for you in the Palace—
  how beautiful is all that is ordered in your Name!

The Two Lands entire are bound to your person,
　　the Nine Bows are under your feet.

And they say, "O divine Ruler (live, prosper, and be healthy),
　　you who love Truth, you who love [kingship]—
There are none who can equal you, none dare to deceive you!
　　there are none who [brush] a single consequence aside;
There is no longer the oppression of falsehood;
　　no placing a rough hand upon Truth;
No need to recite a long list of troubles;
　　there is no striking anyone [on any day]."

O You who make the downstream journeys peaceful fivefold—
　　let good health be to you,
Let life in abundance be yours,
　　and grant us also renewal each day!

60. Hymn to Ramesses II
[On his First Jubilee]

In Praise of the Great Inundation for the first Jubilee of the Horus, User-maat-rê, son of Rê, Ramessu Mery-Amun, given life—when the Nile reached [x] cubits high:

The dikes cannot stand before Hapy!
　　He reaches the mountains!
Lord of the fish, abundant with birds,
　　all his [activities] are beneficial—
He nourishes, all thoughts are sweet,
　　and the very gods make celebration!

Well-pleased is the heart of Egypt in your time!
　　the Black Land shall offer sacrifice daily!
There is no dearth of drinking to satisfaction,
　　and the whole world has come to your throne.
The Ennead of Upper Egypt has gathered
　　to multiply your bounty like the sands;
Your Treasury is filled to overflowing

with every good and shining thing—with fowl and drink;
Incense and wine, there is no room to put them!—
　　your granaries reach the sky.
It is like filling the mouth with cakes
　　that Father Amun bakes for you!

Your excellence is in His heart;
　　and the heart of every god and goddess delights in your
　　　　abilities;
They spend the day and night recounting your accomplishments,
　　their peace of mind rests in your goodness.
You are the king! who wields his mighty arm,
　　who knows how to use his hand,
　　　　strong in his mighty power for those who follow him.

61. In Praise of Ramesses II as a Warrior
[Papyrus Anastasi II]

A good god with the strength of Amun,
　　a sovereign great in his power,
Divine [youth] who came forth from Rê,
　　child of the Bull of Heliopolis;
Who stands there poised, captures with his sturdy arm,
　　like the strong god in the sky-bark, Millions of Years;
A king from his conception, with a majesty like Horus,
　　he seized the world by means of his might;
He made the Two Lands bow to his counsel,
　　and the Nine Bows are trodden under his feet.
All foreign lands are drawn to him bearing their tribute,
　　he puts all nations on a single path without dissent.
The chieftains of the rebel lands are weak,
　　they become like cattle in their terror of him;
He enters in among them like the Son of Nut,
　　and they lie prostrate instantly due to his fiery breath.
Libya is down in slaughter, fallen to his knife;
　　his strength is given him for ever and eternity!
His mighty power enfolds the mountains—
　　O Ramesses Mer-amun (l.p.h.),
　　　　lord of strength, protector of his army.

62. In Praise of Merenptah as Warrior
[Papyrus Anastasi II]

[He is a valiant King], the son of Amun,
    with active arm and fighting heart;
Strong leader who protects his army,
    bull who multiplies [his victories over] all [the lands];
Steady in the chariot of war like the Lord of Thebes,
    mighty guardian [who knows how] to use his hands,
Shooting with strong bow at powerful lions;
    and his strength encompasses each foreign land.
He crosses mountains to seek out those who would attack him,
    his war-cry in their hearts, fear in their faces.
Perfect ruler, vigilant, effective in his counsel,
    may he make his Name victorious throughout the world
As King of Upper and Lower Egypt, Lord of the Two Lands,
    like the majesty of Horus!
The great ones of the nations are bent to your fierce benevolence—
    O Ba-en-rê, Meramun,
        Son of the Sun, Merenptah, at peace in Maat.

63. In Praise of Merenptah
[Papyrus Anastasi II]

The good god who lives on Maat,
    sovereign beloved of the gods,
Precious conception, son of Khepri,
    descendant of the Bull of Heliopolis,
Falcon who enters in the Cartouche,
    child of Isis, Horus,
The Spirit of Rê, sent to appear in Egypt;
    and the land falls into its proper rhythm.

How very mighty is Ba-en-rê (l.p.h.),
    how very apt his counsels!
Whatever he says is effective, like Thoth,
    all he attempts succeeds.
He is like one leading the way before his army,

whose words are a protecting wall.
How beloved is he who bends his back to him,
 to Meryamun, Beloved of Amun (l.p.h.)!

The victorious army has returned
 after it has triumphed in strength and power—
Casting fire on the land of Isderektiw
 burning the country of the Meryna.
The Sherden, whom you carried off through your strong arm,
 have plundered the tribes of the foreign lands.
How delightful is your returning to Thebes—
 your chariot is weighed down with severed hands;
Their chieftains are tied as captives in front of you,
 and you shall soon send them on to your Father,
  Amun Kamutef, Strong Bull of his Mother.

64. A Letter of Homage to Pharaoh Merenptah
[Papyrus Anastasi II]

With life, prosperity, and health! This is for information of the King, residing at the palace, Beloved of Maat, the two horizons of Rê wherein he dwells.

Attend to me, O Shining Light,
 who brightens the Two Lands with his loveliness!
Sundisk of the Sunfolk
 who drives darkness from the Black Land!
You are like the image of your father, Rê,
 who shines down from the heavens;
Your rays penetrate even the underworld
 and no place lacks your beauty.
The affairs of each country are told to you
 while you are at rest in your palace;
And you hear the speech of all nations
 for you have millions of ears.
Brighter your eye than the stars of heaven,
 for you can see more than the sundisk itself.
If one speaks—even a voice from the underworld—

it reaches your ear;
If one does something—and it is concealed—
　　your eye will still observe it,
O Ba-en-rê Meramun (l.p.h.),
　　Lord of compassion who fashions the breath of life.

65. In Praise of Merenptah
[Papyrus Anastasi III]

Ba-en-rê Meramun (l.p.h.) is the foremost ship of the line,
　　a club for beating,
A scimitar for slaying foreigners,
　　A ready javelin.
He came down from the sky, was born in Heliopolis,
　　and he has led to victory in every land.

How beautiful the day is near you,
　　how welcome is your voice in speaking,
As you build the House of Ramesses Meramun (l.p.h.)
　　at the southern border of each foreign land,
　　　　at the far north of Egypt,
With its beautiful windows and gleaming balconies
　　of lapis lazuli and turquoise.
It is the place to drill your chariotry,
　　to field your armies,
To moor your seaborn bowmen
　　who bring you tribute.

Praises to you, as you approach
　　with your companies of archers
　　　　with fearsome faces and hot fingers
Who go out upon the ways of battle
　　after seeing a Ruler (l.p.h.) who is prepared to fight.
The mountains cannot stand before him—
　　they are terrified before your awful presence,
　　　　O Ba-en-rê Meramun.
You will exist while eternity exists,
　　and eternity exists while you do;

May you dwell securely on the throne of your father,
    Rê, the Horus of Twin Horizons.

66. In Praise of the Delta Residence
of Ramesses III
[Papyrus Anastasi II]

Beginning of the Recital of the Power of the Lord of Egypt:

His Majesty (l.p.h.) built himself a country mansion,
    August of Power its name;
It is between Phoenicia and the Delta
    and is filled with food and provisions.

Its plan is like Thebes of Upper Egypt
    and it will outlast the House of Ptah in Memphis.
The Sun rises over its horizon
    and goes to rest within it;
All abandon their home districts
    and settle in its region.
On its western side is the Temple of Amun,
    on the south is the Temple of Seth,
Astarte appears on its east
    and Wadjet to the north.

The Residence within it
    is like the two horizons of the sky;
Ramesses Meramun dwells there as a god,
    Montu of the Nations is his herald,
Rê of the Rulers is vizier—
    and happiness descends on Egypt!
The one beloved of Atum is the mayor,
    and the land has settled into its familiar ways.

The great chieftain of Khatti writes
    addressing the chief of Qedem:
"Get yourself ready that we may hie to Egypt
    to say, 'A miracle of god has happened!'"

And offer flattery to User-maat-rê
    that he may give the breath of life to those he loves."

Each foreign land exists only through love of him;
    Khatti is totally within his awful power—
God will not receive its offerings,
    nor can it spy the rain,
For it is in the power of User-maat-rê (l.p.h.),
    our strong bull who loves valor.

X

From the Schoolboy Miscellanies
Passing on the Religious Tradition

The series of New Kingdom papyri collectively known as "the schoolboy miscellanies" are small anthologies of writings which seem to have been intended for instruction of fledgling scribes in the schools. They are indeed a miscellaneous lot, containing material ranging from proper letter-writing, to descriptions of the lazy scribe, to accounts of how much harder life was in all professions other than that of scribe, to hymns and prayers to gods and kings, like those presented in this section. Much of this material is humdrum; much of it is propaganda by the teaching staff to cajole the young students into working hard to succeed in the profession to which they were apprenticed. The pieces, however, often give vivid pictures of school and scribal life; and at times the writings are quite skillful. The prominence of Thoth in these poems is due to his role as god of writing, guardian of the sacred writings, and protector of scribes and the scribal profession.

67. Prayer to Ptah
"Longing for Memphis"
[Papyrus Anastasi IV]

See how my heart runs off, stealing away!
    It flies to a spot it knows,
Going upstream to see Memphis, House of the Spirit of Ptah—
    and I wish I were with it!
But I sit here expecting my heart back
    so it can tell me how it is in Memphis.

No work can be done by my hand,
　　my mind cannot concentrate.
O come to me, Ptah, to carry me off to Memphis!
　　Let me look about unhindered!
I would spend the day properly
　　but my heart is listless;
My mind will not stay in my body,
　　and misery seizes all of my limbs!
My eye is exhausted with staring,
　　my ear, it will not be filled,
　　　　my voice is hoarse and words become tumbled.
O my Lord, be at peace with me!
　　Help me to rise above all these things!

68. Hymn to Thoth
[Papyrus Anastasi III]

Praises to you, Lord of the Manor,
　　holy baboon with shining mane,
Of pleasing aspect, gentle, charming,
　　loved by all.
To him belongs contentment—for he is Thoth
　　who overwhelms the earth with beauty!

His headdress is red jasper,
　　his phallus is carnelian;
Love gushes out from his eyebrows
　　as he opens his mouth to give life.

My entryway is sweet
　　since the holy creature entered it.
It has developed and is well furnished
　　since my Lord set foot therein.

May you all be happy, you of my neighborhood!
　　Rejoice for me, all my neighbors!
Behold my lord! He made me what I am
　　and my heart belongs to him.
O Thoth, for me you are more than a champion;
　　I shall never fear what you do.

69. Prayer to Thoth
[Papyrus Sallier I]

Chief of the guardians of the archives, Ameneminet, of the Treasury of Pharaoh, writes to the scribe, Pentaweret. This letter is brought to you as follows:

O Thoth, take me to Hermopolis,
    your city where it is pleasant to live,
Providing for my needs of food and drink
    and watching over the words I utter.

If only Thoth would be near me tomorrow!
    "Come!" they say—
And I go into the presence of the Lords of Justice.
    May I come forth vindicated!

O great doum palm sixty cubits high,
    the one with nuts upon it,
With fruit within the nuts
    and water in the fruit:—

O you who can bring water from a faroff place,
    come, rescue me, a thoughtful man!
O Thoth, a well is sweet
    when a man is thirsty in the desert:
It is sealed to one who uncovers his mouth unwisely
    but open to the thoughtful man.
Let the thoughtful man come
    that he may discover the well for the hot-headed man.
        And you shall be filled.

70. Prayer to Thoth
For Wisdom in His Service
[Papyrus Anastasi V]

Come to me, Djehuty! O glorious sacred Ibis,
    god who loves Hermopolis,

Scribe of letters to the Ennead,
    exalted in Heliopolis!
Come to me that you may give good counsel
    and make me wise in your affairs.

Your calling is splendid above any other—
    it makes for greatness;
One discovers the knowledge in it
    to form a distinguished man.

I have seen the many men you favored,
    and they are high officials, seated on the Council of the Thirty,
Strong and powerful because of what you do;
    and it is you who gave them wisdom.
And it is you who give good counsel to him without a mother;
    fate and good fortune are in your hand.

O come to me that you may give me wisdom!
    I am a devotee of your domain.
Let me recount your mighty deeds
    wherever I may be.
Then shall the multitudes of people say,
    "Great are the things Djehuty has accomplished."

Then they shall come bringing their children,
    offering them to your service.
The service of the Lord of Power is perfection!
    And happy he who is allowed to follow it.

71. Prayer to Rê-Horakhty
[Papyrus Anastasi II]

Come to me, O Rê-Horakhty,
    so that you may give me wisdom.
You are the one who accomplishes;
    no one acts without your knowledge—
        rather, you act together with him.
Come to me, Atum, each day;

it is you are the splendid deity.
My heart is gone upstream to Heliopolis;
   my [duties] have fallen away,
     my heart is light, and my thoughts are happy!

Hear my prayers:
   my entreaties of each day
     and my praises in the night.
My petitions shall be increased in my mouth,
   for they are heard this day!
O one alone, O Rê-Horakhty,
   no other here is like him!
Guardian of millions, saving his hundred-thousands,
   protector of any who shall call to him!

O Lord of Heliopolis,
   do not charge me with my myriad wrongs!
I am a man who does not know himself,
   a person without a heart or strength,
Who follows his own dictates
   like an ox pursuing fodder.
As for my nighttime in [. . . . .]
   I take myself about in idleness,
Spending the days wandering in the courtyards
   and the nights [. . . . . .].

[*The rest is lost.*]

72. Praise of Amun-Rê

[Papyrus Anastasi II]

He is Amun-Rê,
   first to act as king,
God of the Beginning Time,
   vizier of the poor.
He does not take bribes from wrongdoers,
   nor speak with one who bears tales,
     nor regard him who makes easy promises.

Amun-Rê judges the earth with his finger,
    and his words shall rest in the heart;
He judges the unjust and sends him on to the Place of Fire;
    the just man goes to the West.

73. Prayer to Amun
Supplication in a Year of Need
[Papyrus Anastasi IV]

Come to me, Amun,
    preserve me in this year of misery!
The sun is up but does not shine,
    winter has come during summer,
Months happen backwards
    and the hours are jumbled.
The eminent cry to you, Amun;
    the humble are seeking you;
And those in the arms of their nurses say,
    "Give us our air, O Amun!"
May Amun find how to come here in peace
    with the sweet breeze before him!
Or may he let me grow wings of protection
    like those bearing his sky-ship.

—Thus speak the herders in countryside fields,
    washermen on the banks of the River,
Medjay-police forsaking their outposts,
    gazelles on the wasting desert.

74. Prayer to Amun
[Papyrus Anastasi IV]

May you find that Amun acts as you desire
    in his hour of benediction
As you are praised within the circle of the magistrates
    and well grounded in the Place of Truth.

O Amun-Rê, your great flood overwhelms the uplands—
    O lord of fish, with many birds—
        and all the poor are fed.

O put the eminent in the seats of the eminent
    and the great in the seats of the great!
And put the Scribe of the Treasury, Kagabu,
    before Djehuty, who is your Truth.

75. Prayer to Amun
Of a Man on Trial
[Papyrus Anastasi II]

Amun, give your ear to one who is alone in court:
    he is needy and without power.
The court extorts him
    with silver and gold for the recording scribes
        and clothing for their followers.
May it be given that Amum transform himself into a vizier,
    allowing this humble man go forth free!
And let it be found that the humble man becomes a just man,
    and let the humble man surpass the powerful.

76. In Praise of Amun
[Papyrus Anastasi II]

A pilot who knows the waters, that is Amun,
    a steering oar for the [helpless],
One who gives food to the one who has not,
    who helps the servant of his house to prosper.

I do not take myself a great man as protector,
    nor do I mingle with the men of means;
I do not place my portion under the strong arm
    of someone wealthy in a [noble] household.

My Lord is my protector,
    I know his strength;
He aids with ready arm and caring look,
    and, all alone, is powerful—

Amun, who knows what kindness is
    and hears the one who cries to him;
Amun, King of the Gods,
    strong Bull who glories in his power.

77. In Praise of Amun
[Papyrus Anastasi IV]

Make glad the heart of Amun in your heart
    that he may lead you to a fine old age.
And may you spend a lifetime of such service
    until you reach the state of blessedness,
Your lips remaining healthy, your limbs sturdy,
    your eye far-gazing, and your clothing fine.

You shall guide a span of horses,
    a staff of gold within your grasp,
A chariot of your own with all new fittings
    and yoked to Syrian steeds,
With Southlanders you have acquired
    running along before you.

You shall embark and travel in your ship of cedar,
    decked out from prow to stern,
Arriving at your splendid country villa
    which you yourself have built.

Your mouth shall be filled with wine and beer,
    with bread, and meat, and baked goods;
With oxen butchered, wine jugs opened,
    and sweet singing in your presence.
Your chief perfumer shall anoint with rich perfumes,
    your chief of irrigated lands bring garlands,
Your overseer of farmers offer fowl,
    and your fishermen give fish.

Your freighters shall return from Khor
    laden with every sort of splendid thing,

Your pens be filled with young,
    and your weavers flourishing.

You shall prosper and your enemy fall,
    the one who spoke against you be no longer.
And you shall enter in the conclave of the Nine Great Gods
    and come forth blest!

═══XI═══

Harper's Songs
In Praise of Life

The harper's songs are difficult to place in the ancient Egyptian religious tradition; for they express the *carpe diem* theme, "seize the day." They celebrate life in this world, taking pleasure while one can; for the end of life is the grave, not a blissful afterlife with Osiris. Their occurrence is puzzling, not because of imprecision in the statement of their theme—that death is the end is clear—but because they are placed in tombs along with other inscriptions, hymns, and prayers which are quite traditional in expressing worship of and hope in the gods of Egypt. The piece from King Intef's tomb (surviving on a papyrus) is thought to go back to the Middle Kingdom; the others belong to the New Kingdom. The three songs from Neferhotep's tomb are particularly revealing, since Neferhotep complains bitterly of the misconceptions of the afterworld disseminated by such pieces as the songs of the harpers.

78. From the Tomb of King Intef
[Papyrus Harris 500]

Song in the tomb of King Intef, vindicated, in front of the singer
with the harp:

He is prospering, this fine prince;
death is a happy ending.

154

i

One generation passes, another stays behind—
    such has it been since the men of ancient times.
The gods of long ago rest in their pyramids,
    and the great and blessed likewise lie buried in their tombs.
Yet those who built great mansions, their places are no more.
    What has become of them all?

I have heard the words of Imhotep, and Hordjedef too,
    retold time and again in their narrations.
Where are their dwellings now?
    Their walls are down,
Their places gone,
    like something that has never been.

There is no return for them
    to explain their present being,
To say how it is with them,
    to gentle our hearts
        until we hasten to the place where they have gone.

ii

So, let your heart be strong,
    let these things fade from your thoughts.
Look to yourself,
    and follow your heart's desire while you live!

Put myrrh on your head,
    be clothed in fine linen,
Anoint yourself with the god's own perfumes,
    heap up your happiness,
        and let not your heart become weary.

Follow your heart's desire and what you find good;
    act on your own behalf while on earth!
And let not your heart be troubled—
    that day of mourning for you must come;
And Osiris, the Weary-Hearted, will not hear their wailing,
    weeping does not save the heart from the grave.

So spend your days joyfully
and do not be weary with living!
No man takes his things with him,
and none who go can come back again.

79. From the Tomb of Inherkhawy
[Theban Tomb 359]

Sung by the harpist of the osiris, Chief of the Crew in the Place of Truth,
Inherkhawy, vindicated, who says, "I was an eminent person and a man
redeemed through abundance of good offered by God himself."

The forms which come into being as flesh
pass on, and have since the time of the god;
and the young are come into their places.
The transfigured spirits who live in the afterworld,
and those made into stars as well,
And those who built their mansions—and tombs—
all, all are at rest in their graves.

So build a great home in the land of the dead
that your name may endure because of it;
Count up your works in the realm under god
so your seat in the West may be splendid!
The waters flow north, the wind blows south,
and each man goes to his hour.

So spend the day happily, O osiris,
chief of the crew in the Place of Truth,
Inherkhawy, triumphant.
Do not be weary at all, having what is dear to you with you,
do no harm to your heart during your time upon earth.
Spend the day happily, happily;
take finest sweetgums gathered beside you,
with garlands of blossoming flowers at your breast.
And the woman within your heart, your beloved,
gives joy as she sits beside you.

Be not troubled at heart over all that happens,
    let there be singing before you;
Recall not the evil, hateful to God,
    but always remember joy.

O upright man, straightforward and true,
    patient, kind-hearted, content with your lot,
        joyful, not speaking evil—
Let your heart be drunk on the gifts of the day
    until that day comes when you anchor.

80. Three Harper's Songs
From the Tomb of Neferhotep
[Theban Tomb 50]

i. First Song

Chanted by the singer with the harp for the God's Father of Amun, Neferhotep, vindicated:

O all you excellent eminent dead, O Ennead, O Lady of Life
    in the West,
    hear what has been composed
To sing the praises of the God's Father in honoring his soul,
    what is helpful for the excellent dead man
Now that he is a living god for eternity,
    elevated in the West.
May these words become a memorial in future
    to anyone who passes by.

I have heard those songs in the tombs of ancient days
    and what they say, exalting life on earth
        and belittling the city of the dead.
Why is this, acting this way against the land of eternity
    which is just and without terror?
It loathes disorder;
    and no one arms himself against a neighbor
        in this land without a rebel.

All our ancestors have come to rest within it
>   since the wastes at the beginning of time;
And those who shall come to be, millions on millions,
>   all go there.
There is no lingering in our Beloved Land,
>   not one fails to arrive there;
And the span of what was done on earth is the flicker of a dream
>   when they say, "Welcome, safe and sound!"
>   to the one who reaches the West.

ii. Second Song

Beginning of the song:

Recall, O heart, that fearful day of mooring;
>   place it firmly in the minds of all who shall be buried!
O [do not fail] to give it honor,
>   for, surely, none escape.
Strong and weak are in the same condition;
>   whether they travel up or down the River during life,
>   it is there they moor at last.

O God's Father, what a fine lot is yours
>   that you have joined the lords of eternity!
How enduring is your name forevermore
>   as one transfigured in the Land of God.
The gods you followed when you were alive—
>   you have the entrée to them face to face;
They are ready to receive your soul, preserve your honors,
>   and multiply the good works of your hands;
They shall purify your beauty
>   and maintain the altar to your person,
>   each god with his portion.
And they say to you,
>   "Welcome in peace, O priest pleasing to our spirit!"
—For the God's Father Neferhotep,
>   begotten of the noble man, Ameneminet.

O God's Father, let me hear your praises before the Lords
>   of Eternity:

they say, "He has drawn the bark of Sokar!"—
May you place the hastening god in his sledge
    and circle the walls, following him of the shining breast.
"He has raised up the Djed-pillar like a sem-priest at his duty,
    taken the hoe on the days for tilling earth,
Recited the ritual of Busiris."
    Blessed be your existence with the gods!
You shall be remembered for your accomplishments;
    and it is you who can enter Heliopolis, knowing its Mysteries.
—For the lector-priest who satisfies the heart of Amun,
    Neferhotep, vindicated.

O God's Father, your soul advances
    and your coffin passes by.
Anubis seeks you out, his arms about you;
    the Two Sisters embrace you;
The purifying rites are once again performed for you,
    for you are now entrusted with the labors of eternity.
[You have] the likeness of a god,
    anointed by the hands of Shezemu,
Clothed through the labors of Tayt—
    with the Sons of Horus as your whole protection.
For you the Twin Kites sit at the Twin Gates
    to cry out lamentations in your Name.
Daily, your life on earth is beneficial to your Lord Amun,
    O God's Father of Amun, Neferhotep, vindicated.

O God's Father, the memory of you endures in Heliopolis,
    your authority remains in Thebes.
Never can it be that you are lost through all eternity
    nor shall your Name be gone—
Because you are one who was just in the House of Ptah,
    who could enter face to face at the Great Throne.
One wise in the ways of the god's appearances,
    one deep in the knowledge of time and of eternity.

Be raised up, glorious in your heightened being,
    O honored Neferhotep, vindicated
(Whose son is vindicated too)—
    whose enemies are overthrown for all eternity.

iii. Third Song

Spoken by the singer with the harp who is in the tomb of the osiris and
God's Father of Amun, Neferhotep, vindicated. He says:

How restful is this righteous man!
    What had to come has turned out well!

Generations have passed on since the time of the god,
    and the young come into their places.
Rê offers himself at dawn,
    and Atum sinks to rest in the Western Mountain.
Men beget, women conceive,
    and every nostril inhales the breeze.
At dawn they are born one after another,
    then they all go on to the place set aside.

Live happily, O God's Father!
    Take fine perfumes pleasing to your nostrils,
With garlands, lotuses, and berries at your breast,
    with your beloved, who is in your heart, happy at your side.
Put singing and music before you;
    turn your back on every sadness
Remember only joy
    until the coming of that day wherein one moors
In the land that loves silence
    where the heart of the Son who loves Him never wearies.
Spend the day happily, Neferhotep, vindicated,
    O God's Father, excellent, with pure hands!

I have heard the things which happened to those of former days—
    their homes destroyed, their places gone,
As if they had never been since the time of the god.
    [Those lords] abandoned what are now your fields,
Your soul now occupies their possessions,
    drinking their waters and refreshing your heart.

Offer bread to him who is without his land
    that a good name may be yours in future and eternity.
The [watching eyes of their descendants] look to you—

their offerings are gone, their bread is stale,
   their harpists sing [no more].

Raise up their sacred figures to the throne of Rê!
   Their people cry out in their misery;
[They] cannot do [their work] while coming to their end,
   and Destiny counts off his days.
Awaken [to his] situation—
   the wretched man who must be servant to his Shade.

Live happily , O thou pure of hand,
   God's Father, Neferhotep!

[*From here on the text is too fragmentary to translate.*]

XII

Love Songs
In Praise of Love

The love songs of the New Kingdom are quite different in flavor from all the other selections in this volume; for they are secular. Certainly the moods of worship and adulation are there; but in this case the object is not a god or a king but a boy or a girl, sometimes a man or a woman. These songs are a precious inheritance from the lyric poetry of ancient Egypt since they give the modern reader a glimpse of the intimate feelings and attitudes of young lives full of passion and longing, intrigue and duplicity, love and sadness. These few love songs—there are only about sixty of them—show another side of the lyric voice of ancient Egypt; they give a kind of cross-light to the picture of the ancient Egyptian as totally religious; for nothing could be further from the truth. The ancient Egyptian could love the gods and the king while reserving a special place in the heart for one or more human creatures.

81
[Papyrus Chester Beatty I, recto]

[*He speaks:*]

What is my love trying to do to me?
  Am I to keep quiet about it?
Making me stand at the door of her house
  while she gets herself inside!

Not even saying, "Have a nice trip home!"
    Why, she dammed up her ears the whole night!

82
[Papyrus Chester Beatty I, recto]

[*She speaks:*]

Why do you question your heart?
    After her! I say. Take her tight in your arms!
For god's sake, it's me coming at you,
    my tunic over my shoulder!

83
[Papyrus Chester Beatty I, verso]

[*He speaks:*]

My love is one alone, without her equal,
    beautiful above all women.
See her, like the goddess of the morning star in splendor
    at the beginning of a happy year.

With dazzling presence and a fair complexion,
    with lovely watching eyes,
With lips that are sweet in speaking,
    and not a word too much;
Straight her neck and white her breast,
    and her tresses gleam like lapis lazuli;
Her arms are more precious than gold,
    her fingers like lotus blossoms,
With curving hips and a trim waist,
    and thighs that only heighten her beauty.
Her step is pleasing as she treads upon earth;
    and she fastens my heart in her embrace.
She makes the necks of the young men
    swing round about to see her.

Happy is he who can fully embrace her—
    he is first of all the young lovers!
Just look at her as she walks along,
    like that goddess beyond, One alone!

84
[Papyrus Chester Beatty I, verso]

[*She speaks:*]

My heart was intending to go and see Nefrus
    and sit awhile at her house;
But I found Mehy riding down the road
    along with his band of young men.
I did not know how to escape him
    in order to get by him unhindered.
Oh look! the path is like the River—
    there is no place to put my feet!

My heart is so foolish:
    "Why avoid Mehy?"
Oh, if I go near him
    I shall tell him my wavering heart.
"I am yours!" I would say to him.
    And he would shout out my name
And put me away in the finest harem
    of all those meant for his servants.

85. The Memphis Ferry
[Papyrus Harris 500]

[*He speaks:*]

I am going downstream on the ferry
    under the [guiding hand] of the captain,
        my bundle of old clothes on my shoulder.

I am headed for Memphis, Life of the Two Lands,
    and I shall say to Ptah, Lord of Justice,
      "Give me a girl in the night!"

The water is full of vegetation—
    Ptah is the reeds,
      Sakhmet the lotus shoots,
The goddess of dew is the lotus buds,
    and Nefertem the blossoms,
      [. . . . . .]

When day dawns in all its loveliness,
    Memphis will be a gift of berries
      offered the god of the handsome face.

86
[Papyrus Harris 500]

[*He speaks:*]

I shall go lie down at home,
    and I shall feign sickness.
Then the neighbors will enter to look at me,
    and my love will come with them.
She will force the doctors to leave defeated—
    for she knows my malady!

87. Songs of the Birdcatcher's Daughter, ii
[Papyrus Harris 500]

[*She speaks:*]

The voice of the wild goose cries out,
    caught by his bait-worm;
And love of you ensnares me—
    I do not know how to work free.

I must gather my nets;
     but what in the world shall I tell mother,
Returning to her each day
     loaded down with my catch?
I shall be setting no trap today;
     I am taken myself—by love of you.

88. Songs of the Birdcatcher's Daughter, iii
[Papyrus Harris 500]

[*She speaks:*]

The wild goose flies up, then settles,
     diving into the netting;
Birds scurry about like lizards,
     and I hurry [to calm them.]
I turn back bearing my love for you,
     for I am alone—
This heart of mine is counterpart to your own;
     I shall never be far from your charms.

89. Songs of the Birdcatcher's Daughter, vi
[Papyrus Harris 500]

[*She speaks:*]

The voice of the swallow is calling,
     saying, "Land is alight. What is your path?"
O little bird, cease your chattering,
     for I found my love in his bed;
And my heart was overjoyed
     when he said to me, "I shall never be far;
But hand in hand we shall walk,
     and I shall be with you in each happy place."
He put me first of his favorite girls!
     —he would never injure my heart.

XIII

Other Poems

This final section is devoted to three small poems which do not conveniently fit elsewhere. The first is a song commemorating a military victory. It appears in the Dynasty 6 tomb of Weni and is interesting because of its verse structure (a litany) and because it is one of the earliest pieces of secular poetry to have survived. The prayer of King Ramesses II to his father, the god Amun, is an excerpt from the mini-epic "Battle of Kadesh," and is a fine poem in its own right. And finally, there is the litany-like piece praising the teacher, at the same time demonstrating how different the ancient Egyptian priest-instructor was from today's college or university professor.

90. Victory Song of Weni
[Cairo Museum Stele 1435]

This army returned in triumph
    after destroying the land of the bedouin;
This army returned in triumph
    after leveling the land of the sandfarers;
This army returned in triumph
    after tearing down its sanctuaries;
This army returned in triumph
    after cutting down its fig trees and vines;
This army returned in triumph
    after setting fire to all its dwellings;
This army returned in triumph

after killing the troops in it by the tens of thousands;
This army returned in triumph
    after taking a great multitude of the troops therein as captives.

And I was praised by his Majesty for it above anything.

91. Prayer of Ramesses II
At the Battle of Kadesh, 1275 B.C.E.

Then said his Majesty:

What is this with you, my Father Amun?
    What sort of father ignores his son?
        My plans collapse without you.
Have I not gone and listened for your voice
    that I might not disobey the counsel which you gave?
—How great he is, the mighty Lord of Egypt,
    letting foreigners encroach upon his lands!—
What is on your mind?
    These Asiatics are hiding scoundrels ignorant of god!

Have I not constructed for you many towering monuments?
    Did I not fill your temples with my spoils of war?
Did I not build for you my House of Millions of Years
    and give you all my goods as legacy?
Did I not govern for you each land entire
    in order to provide your offerings?
Did I not present to you some thirty thousand oxen
    along with many plants and flowers of sweet aroma?
Did I not turn from the good that would be mine
    in order to complete the buildings in your courtyard?
Did I not raise you mighty gates of stone
    and set their flags myself?
Did I not bring you obelisks from Abu?
    And it was I who furnished workers skilled in stone!
Did I not bring over ships from the Great Green Sea
    in order to convey to you the work of foreign lands?

Might One consider then a small good deed
    in favor of the one who trusts himself to your good counsel?
Do good to him who counts on you;
    then he obeys you with a heart of love!

I have cried out to you, my father Amun,
    amidst a multitude of enemies I do not know.
The foreign lands assembled fight against me,
    I am alone, there is no other with me.
My host of infantry has gone,
    nor did a single charioteer look back at me
        as I cried out to them;
Not one heard me
    as I called to them.

But then I found Amun mighty for me
    above a million soldiers, a hundred thousand charioteers,
More than ten thousand men, comrades and children,
    united in singleness of heart.
No, not the work of multitudes of people—
    Amun is mightier than they!
I learned these things from your own mouth, O Amun;
    and I did not exceed your counsel.

So, I prayed at the far end of the world,
    and my voice echoed through Thebes;
And I found that Amun would come
    once I cried out to him.
He put his hand in mine
    and I was happy.
And he called as if behind me,
    "Go forward! I am with you!
        I am your Father, my hand is in yours!
I am stronger than hundreds of thousands of men!
    I am the Lord of Battle, Lover of Victory!"

And I found that my heart was steadied,
    and my mind was filled with joy;
All I was doing turned out well,
    and I attacked like Montu!

92. A Litany in Praise of the Teacher
[Papyrus Lansing]

You have skilled hands bearing the censer
    before the Lord of the Gods each time he appears.
You are a God's Father, Overseer of the Mysteries,
    carrying the fan in your right hand and the royal linen
        in your left,
      with the Hand-of-Shu in your grasp to glorify your Lord.
You are an august high-priest in the temple of Ptah,
    one wise in all the secret things of the House of the Prince.
You are burial-priest of Kamutef,
    Greatest of Seers of Rê at Thebes, presiding over his offerings.

You are wide-striding on the day of the festival of Sokar,
    one admitting people of Ta-mery to your lord who bears
      the flail.
Your arms are skilled at bearing the water-jar,
    offering libations, censing, and reciting the invocations.
You are deft of hand at the reversion of offerings,
    first to invoke praise in the daily offering.
You are the one who embraces the holy Eye of Mut, Mistress
    of Heaven,
    on the first day of ferrying her about within her precinct
    of Asheru.
You are the one who draws the water for Khonsu in Thebes,
    on the day of the reversion-offerings in the House
    of the Prince.

You are wise in counsel, apt in speaking,
    always looking ahead—and whatever you do succeeds.
You are a judge of hearts—like the divine Ibis;
    curious about all matters, as are the Eye and Ear.
You are powerful, good to your dependants;
    your food offerings are abundant like a high Nile.
You are rich in provisions, knowing how to dispense them
    to all whom you love like a swelling sea.

You are an eminent, even-tempered man, offspring of the
    praiseworthy,

beloved of all who bear the favor of the king.
You have been of high station since your birth,
    and your hall is flooded with abundance.
You are rich in fields, with well-stocked granaries;
    grain has accrued to you since the day of your birth.
You are blessed with horses, bright with sails;
    your ships gleam like red jasper on the flood.
You have many crews wise in navigation,
    their words are pleasant as they carry and load.

You are judicious, careful in your answers;
    you have hated coarse speech since your birth.
You are handsome, pleasantly formed,
    and love of you fills everyone like a high Nile.
You are discriminating in speech, skilled in what is said;
    whatever you say is accurate—and you hate lying.
You sit majestically within your hall,
    your servants answer speedily,
Those who pour the ale pour furiously,
    and all who see you are festive with happiness!

You serve your lord well, you help dependants flourish;
    all that comes from your mouth is pleasing to the mind.
You are one who, when you give the beer-jug, fills it full;
    beloved of Him who drives the cattle at the offering;
And you direct the Jubilee Festival for the Sovereign—
    He who puts the Nine Bows at his feet and cares for his army.

Sources

1.   **Text:** Sethe 1908: 1:205–16.
      Translations: Faulkner 1969: 80–84; Lichtheim 1973: 1:36–38; Simpson, Faulkner, and Wente 1973: 269–73; Foster 1992: 19–23.
2.   **Text:** Sethe 1908: 1:426–32.
      Translation: Faulkner 1969: 141–43.
3.   **Text:** Sethe 1908: 1:292–93.
      Translations: Faulkner 1969: 112; Lichtheim 1973: 1:41.
4.   **Text:** Sethe 1908: 1:137–38.
      Translations: Faulkner 1969: 58; Lichtheim 1973: 1:32–33.
5.   **Text:** Sethe 1908: 1:358–62.
      Translations: Faulkner 1969: 123–24; Lichtheim 1973: 1:41–42.
6.   **Text:** Sethe 1908: 2:142–49.
      Translation: Faulkner 1969: 187–88.
7.   **Text:** Sethe 1908: 2:127–31.
      Translation: Faulkner 1969: 184–85.
8.   **Text:** Sethe 1908: 1:387–91.
      Translations: Faulkner 1969: 133; Lichtheim 1973: 1:43–44.
9.   **Text:** Sethe 1908: 1:161–66.
      Translation: Faulkner 1969: 67.
10.   **Text:** Sethe 1908: 1:280–81.
      Translations: Faulkner 1969: 109; Lichtheim (1973): 1:40–41.
11.   **Text:** Sethe 1908: 2:80–83.
      Translations: Faulkner 1969: 173; Lichtheim 1973: 1:47–48.
12.   **Text:** Sethe 1908: 1:199–202.
      Translations: Faulkner 1969: 78–79; Lichtheim 1973: 1:35–36.

13. **Text:** Sethe 1908: 1:181–83.
     Translations: Faulkner 1969: 72–73; Lichtheim 1973: 1:34–35.
14. **Text:** Sethe 1908: 1:253–54.
     Translations: Faulkner 1969: 96; Lichtheim 1973: 1:39.
15. **Text:** Sethe 1908: 1:174–75.
     Translation: Faulkner 1969: 70.
16. **Text:** Sethe 1908: 1:85–86.
     Translation: Faulkner 1969: 43–44.
17. **Text:** Sethe 1908: 2:308–13.
     Translation: Faulkner 1969: 228–229.
18. **Text:** Sethe 1908: 1:195–99.
     Translation: Faulkner 1969: 76–77.
19. **Text:** Sethe 1908: 2:389–97.
     Translation: Faulkner 1969: 250–51.
20. **Text:** Sethe 1908: 2:358–60.
     Translation: Faulkner 1969: 243.
21. **Text:** Sethe 1908: 2:344–55.
     Translation: Faulkner 1969: 238–41.
22. **Text:** Sethe 1908: 1:474–79.
     Translation: Faulkner 1969: 151–52.
23. **Text:** Sethe 1908: 2:372–77.
     Translation: Faulkner 1969: 246–47.
24. **Text:** *The Epigraphic Survey* 1980: Pl. 20.
     Translations: Wente 1980: 38; Assmann 1975: 162–64 (#56).
25. **Text:** *The Epigraphic Survey* 1980: Pl. 7.
     Translation: Wente 1980: 30–32.
26. **Text:** Martin 1989: Pl. 25.
     Translation: Martin 1989: 33–34.
27. **Text:** Martin 1989: Pls. 21–22.
     Translations: Martin 1989: 29–31; Barucq and Daumas 1980: 122–124
     (#24) and 352–53 (#95); Assmann 1975: 165–69 (#58).
28. **Text:** Moret 1931: 725–30 and Pls. I–III.
     Translations: Barucq and Daumas 1980: 91–97 (#11); Assmann 1975:
     443–48 (#213); Lichtheim 1976: 2:81–86; Foster 1992: 40–46.
29. **Text:** *The Epigraphic Survey* 1980: Pl. 19.
     Translation: Wente 1980: 37.
30. **Text:** Edwards 1939: 22–25 and Pl. xxi; Sethe 1927–30: 1943–47; De
     Buck 1963: 113–15.
     Translations: Barucq and Daumas 1980: 187–91 (#68); Assmann 1975:
     209–12 (#89); Lichtheim 1976: 2:86–89.

31. **Text:** Mariette 1872: 2: Pls. xi–xiii. Cf. G. Möller, *Hieratische Lesestücke* 2: Pls. 33–34 (sections i–vi only).
    Translations: Barucq and Daumas 1980: 191–201 (#69); Assmann 1975: 199–207 (#87).
32. **Text:** Golénischchev 1927: 169–96.
    Translations: Barucq and Daumas 1980: 255–61 (#79); Assmann 1975: 308–12 (#131).
33. **Text:** Zandee 1947: passim.
    Translations: Barucq and Daumas 1980: 206–29 (#72); Assmann 1975: 312–21 (#132–42, selections only); Foster 1992: 63–79, selections.
34. **Text:** Budge 1910: 1:1–3.
    Translation: Faulkner 1985: 27; Assmann 1975: 133–35 (#29–30).
35. **Text:** Budge 1910: 1:3–5.
    Translation: In part: Barucq and Daumas 1980: 168–69 (#61).
36. **Text:** Budge 1910: 1:6–7.
    Translation: Barucq and Daumas 1980: 170–72 (#62–63).
37. **Text:** Budge 1910: 1:7–9.
    Translations: Barucq and Daumas 1980: 174–77 (#65); Assmann 1975: 146–48 (#42A–B).
38. **Text:** Budge 1910: 1:10–11.
    Translation: None.
39. **Text:** Budge 1910: 1:36–38.
    Translations: Faulkner 1985: 40; Barucq and Daumas 1980: 172–74 (#64); Assmann 1975: 135–37 (#31–32).
40. **Text:** Budge 1910: 1:40–45.
    Translations: Faulkner 1985: 41–44; Assmann 1975: 139–44 (#34–39).
41. **Text:** Budge 1910: 1:45–48.
    Translation: None.
42. **Text:** Budge 1910: 1:48–50.
    Translation: Assmann 1975: 150–51 (#44).
43. **Text:** Budge 1910: 1:12–13.
    Translation: None.
44. **Text:** Budge 1910: 1:38–40.
    Translations: Assmann 1975: 137–39 (#33); Faulkner 1985: 40–41.
45. **Texts:** Davies 1908: 6: Pls. 27 and 41; Sandman 1938: 93–96.
    Translations: Lichtheim 1976: 2:96–100; Assmann 1975: 215–21 (#92); Foster 1992: 5–10.
46. **Text:** Erichsen 1933: 49–50.
    Translations: Barucq and Daumas 1980: 388–89 (#117: hymn only); Assmann 1975: 414–15 (#199: hymn only).

47. **Text:** Helck 1955–58: 2090–91.
    Translation: Lichtheim 1976: 2:101.
48. **Text:** Helck 1955–58: 2091–94.
    Translations: Lichtheim 1976: 2:102–3; Assmann 1975: 463–65 (#222).
49. **Text:** Helck 1955–58: 2089–90.
    Translations: Lichtheim 1976: 2:101.
50. **Text:** Martin 1989: Pl. 22, lines 18–25.
    Translations: Martin 1989: 31; Barucq and Daumas 1980: 352–53 (#95); Assmann 1975: 168–69, vv. 69–93 (#58).
51. **Text:** Van der Plas 1986: 2: passim. Eclectic Text: Foster 1975: 1–29.
    Translations: Van der Plas 1986; Lichtheim 1973: 1: 204–10; Foster 1992: 47–52.
52. **Text:** Posener 1938–80: 3: Pls. 81–84a.
    Translation: Fischer-Elfert 1986: 31–62.
53. **Text:** Davies 1953: 3: Pl. 12.
    Translation: Barucq and Davies 1980: 461–64 (#141).
54. **Text:** Gardiner 1931: Pls. XXIV–XXIVA.
    Translations: Barucq and Daumas 1980: 441–42; Lichtheim 1976: 2:184; Simpson, Faulkner, and Wente 1973: 319; Foster 1974: 54–55.
55. **Text:** Tylor and Griffith 1894: Pl. IX; Sethe 1927–30: 1:111–23.
    Translation: Tylor and Griffith 1894: 27–31; Lichtheim 1976: 2:15–21.
56. **Text:** Foster 1993: 10–12.
    Translations: Assmann 1975: 474–76 (#227); Lichtheim 1973: 1:225–26; Simpson, Faulkner, and Wente 1973: 61–62; Foster 1992: 89–91.
57. **Text:** Foster 1993: 33–34.
    Translations: Lichtheim 1973: 1:232; Simpson, Faulkner, and Wente 1973: 72; Foster 1992: 104.
58. **Text:** Griffith 1898: Pls. I–IV.
    Translations: Assmann 1975: 476–80 (#228–31); Lichtheim 1973: 1:198–210; Simpson, Faulkner, and Wente 1973: 279–84.
59. **Text:** Foster 1994: 87–97.
    Translation: Foster 1994: 94.
60. **Text:** Černy and Gardiner 1957: Pls. IX–IXa; and Oriental Institute Chicago Ostracon 19265 (unpublished).
    Translation: Barucq and Daumas 1980: 504–6 (#158).
61. **Text:** Gardiner 1937: 13.
    Translation: Caminos 1954: 40–43.
62. **Text:** Gardiner 1937: 14.
    Translation: Caminos 1954: 43–44.

63. **Text:** Gardiner 1937: 14–15.
    Translation: Caminos 1954: 44–47.
64. **Text:** Gardiner 1937: 15–16.
    Translations: Caminos 1954: 48–50; Barucq and Daumas 1980: 488–89 (#155); Assmann 1975: 497 (#240).
65. **Text:** Gardiner 1937: 28–29.
    Translation: Caminos 1954: 101–3.
66. **Text:** Gardiner 1937: 12–13.
    Translation: Caminos 1954: 37–40.
67. **Text:** Gardiner 1937: 39.
    Translations: Caminos 1957: 150–52; Foster 1992: 60.
68. **Text:** Gardiner 1937: 25.
    Translations: Caminos 1954: 88–91; Barucq and Daumas 1980: 360–61 (#100).
69. **Text:** Gardiner 1937: 85–86.
    Translations: Caminos 1954: 321–23; Barucq and Daumas 1980: 359–60 (#99); Assmann 1975: 384–85 (#182); Lichtheim 1976: 2:114.
70. **Text:** Gardiner 1937: 60.
    Translations: Caminos 1954: 232–34; Barucq and Daumas 1980: 362–63 (#101); Assmann 1975: 356–57 (#151); Lichtheim 1976: 2:113.
71. **Text:** Gardiner 1937: 18–19.
    Translations: Caminos 1954: 60–63; Barucq and Daumas 1980: 145–46 (#42); Assmann 1975: 380 (#176).
72. **Text:** Gardiner 1937: 2, 16.
    Translations: Caminos 1954: 9–10, 50; Barucq and Daumas 1980: 253 (#78A); Assmann 1975: 379 (#174); Lichtheim 1976: 2:111.
73. **Text:** Gardiner 1937: 45.
    Translations: Caminos 1954: 170–74; Barucq and Daumas 1980: 254–55 (#78D); Assmann 1975: 382 (#179); Foster 1992: 59.
74. **Text:** Gardiner 1937: 45–46.
    Translations: Caminos 1954: 174–76; Barucq and Daumas 1980: 255 (#78E); Assmann 1975: 383 (#180).
75. **Text:** Gardiner 1937: 17.
    Translations: Caminos 1954: 56–58; Barucq and Daumas 1980: 253–54 (#78B); Assmann 1975: 379 (#175); Lichtheim 1976: 2:111.
76. **Text:** Gardiner 1937: 17–18.
    Translations: Caminos 1954: 58–60; Barucq and Daumas 1980: 254 (#78C); Assmann 1975: 380–81 (#177); Lichtheim 1976: 2:112.
77. **Text:** Gardiner 1937: 37–38.
    Translation: Caminos 1954: 137–43.

78. **Text:** Fox 1985: 378–80.
   Translations: Lichtheim 1973: 1:194–97; Simpson 1973: 306–7.
79. **Text:** Bruyére 1930: Pls. XXII,3 and XXIII, p. 70.
   Translations: Lichtheim 1945: 201; Foster 1992: 80–81.
80. **Text:** Hari 1985: Pls. IV, XXVI.
   Translations: Hari 1985: i: pp. 12–13; ii: pp. 14–15; iii: pp. 37–39; Lichtheim 1976: 2:115–16 (first song only).
81. **Text:** Gardiner 1931: Pl. XVII, pp. 6–7.
   Translations: Lichtheim 1976: 2:188 (#6); Simpson, Faulkner, and Wente 1973: 324–25 (#46); Foster 1974: 12; Fox 1985: 75 (#46).
82. **Text:** Gardiner 1931: Pl. XVII, 3–4.
   Translations: Lichtheim 1976: 2:188 (#4); Simpson, Faulkner, and Wente 1973: 324 (#44); Foster 1974: 9; Fox 1985: 74 (#44).
83. **Text:** Gardiner 1931: Pl. XXII, 1–9.
   Translations: Lichtheim 1976: 2:182; Simpson, Faulkner, and Wente 1973: 315–16 (#31); Foster 1974: 45–46; Fox 1985: 52 (#31).
84. **Text:** Gardiner 1931: Pl. XXIII, 4–9.
   Translations: Lichtheim 1976: 2:183; Simpson, Faulkner, and Wente 1973: 317–18; Foster 1974: 50–51; Fox 1985: 53 (#33).
85. **Text:** Fox 1985: 372.
   Translations: Lichtheim 1976: 2:189 (#5); Simpson, Faulkner, and Wente 1973: 299–300 (#5); Foster 1974: 71; Fox 1985: 11–12 (#5).
86. **Text:** Fox 1985: 372–73.
   Translations: Lichtheim 1976: 2:189 (#6); Simpson, Faulkner, and Wente 1973: 300 (#6); Foster 1974: 72; Fox 1985: 13 (#6).
87. **Text:** Fox 1985: 375–76.
   Translations: Lichtheim 1976: 2:190 (#2); Simpson, Faulkner, and Wente 1973: 303 (#10); Foster 1974: 102; Fox 1985: 19 (#10).
88. **Text:** Fox 1985: 376.
   Translations: Lichtheim 1976: 2:190 (#3); Simpson, Faulkner, and Wente 1973: 303 (#11); Foster 1974: 104; Fox 1985: 20 (#11).
89. **Text:** Fox 1985: 377.
   Translations: Lichtheim 1976: 2:190–91 (#6); Simpson, Faulkner, and Wente 1973: 304–5 (#14); Foster 1974: 108; Fox 1985: 23 (#14).
90. **Text:** Sethe 1933: 103–4.
   Translation: Lichtheim 1973: 1:20.
91. **Text:** Kitchen 1975–90: 2:34–44.
   Translation: Lichtheim 1976: 2:65–66.
92. **Text:** Gardiner 1937: 112–15.
   Translations: Caminos 1954: 419–26; Lichtheim 1976: 2:173–75.

Bibliography

Aldred, Cyril
1987   *The Egyptians*. New York: Thames & Hudson.
Allen, Thomas George
1960   *The Egyptian Book of the Dead: Documents in the Oriental Institute Museum at the University of Chicago*. Oriental Institute Publications 82. Chicago: University of Chicago Press.
Annual Egyptological Bibliography
1947–   Currently compiled by L. M. J. Zonhoven et al. Leiden: Nederlands Instituut voor het Nabije Oosten. Annually since 1947; now through 1992.
Assmann, Jan
1975   *Ägyptische Hymnen und Gebete*. Zurich and Munich: Artemis Verlag.
1995   *Egyptian Solar Religion: Re, Amun and the Crisis of Polytheism*. Translated by Anthony Alcock. London and New York: Kegan Paul International.
Baines, John, and Jaromír Málek
1980   *Atlas of Ancient Egypt*. London: Phaidon Press.
Barucq, André, and François Daumas
1980   *Hymnes et Prieres de l'Égypte Ancienne*. Littératures Anciennes du Proche-Orient. Paris: Cerf.
Bonnet, Hans
1952   *Reallexikon der ägyptischen Religionsgeschichte*. 2nd ed. Berlin: Walter de Gruyter.
Bruyére, B.
1930   *Fouilles de l'Institut Français d'Archéologie Orientale* VIII, fasc. iii, Plates XXII,3 and XXIII, p. 70. Cairo: Institut Française d'Archéologie Orientale.

Budge, E. A. Wallis

1910   *The Chapters of Coming Forth by Day or the Theban Recension of the Book of the Dead. The Egyptian Hieroglyphic Text Edited from Numerous Papyri.* 4 vols. (with Vocabulary). Books on Egypt and Chaldea. London: Kegan Paul, Trench, Trübner & Co., 1910. Reprint, AMS Press, 1976.

Caminos, Ricardo A.

1954   *Late-Egyptian Miscellanies.* London: Oxford Univesity Press.

Černy, Jaroslav, and Alan Gardiner

1957   *Hieratic Ostraca.* Oxford: Oxford University Press.

Davies, Norman de Garis

1908   *The Rock Tombs of el Amarna. Part VI.–Tombs of Parennefer, Tutu, and Aÿ.* Archeological Survey of Egypt, Eighteenth Memoir. London: Egypt Exploration Fund. Reprinted 1975.

1953   *The Temple of Hibis III.* New York: Metropolitan Museum of Art Egyptian Expedition.

De Buck, A.

1963   *Egyptian Readingbook.* Leiden: Nederlands Instituut voor het Nabije Oosten.

Edwards, I. E. S.

1939   *Hieroglyphic Texts from Egyptian Stelae etc.* Vol. 8. London: British Museum.

Edwards, I. E. S., C. J. Gadd, and N. G. L. Hammond, eds.

1970–   *The Cambridge Ancient History,* 3rd ed., vols. I–II. Cambridge: Cam-
75   bridge University Press.

Epigraphic Survey, The

1980   *The Tomb of Kheruef: Theban Tomb 192.* Oriental Institute Publications 102. Chicago: The Oriental Institute of the University of Chicago.

Erichsen, W.

1933   *Papyrus Harris I: Hieroglyphische Transkription.* Bibliotheca Aegyptiaca 5. Bruxelles: La Fondation Égyptologique Reine Élisabeth.

Erman, Adolf

1927   *The Ancient Egyptians: A Sourcebook of their Writings.* Translated by Aylward M. Blackman. New York: Harper & Row Introduction to the Torchbook edition, 1966, by William Kelly Simpson.

Erman, Adolf, and Hermann Grapow, eds.

1926–   *Wörterbuch der ägyptischen Sprache.* Leipzig: J. C. Hinrichs.
31   Reprinted 1971.

Faulkner, R. O.
1962   *A Concise Dictionary of Middle Egyptian.* Oxford, Griffith Institute.
1969   *The Ancient Egyptian Pyramid Texts.* Oxford: Oxford University Press.
1985   *The Ancient Egyptian Book of the Dead.* Rev. ed. Edited by Carol Andrews. New York: Macmillan Publishing Co.

Fischer-Elfert, Hans-Werner
1986   *Literarische Ostraka der Ramessidenzeit in Übersetzung.* Kleine Ägyptische Texte. Wiesbaden: Otto Harrassowitz.

Foster, John L.
1974   *Love Songs of the New Kingdom.* New York: Charles Scribner's Sons. Reprint, Austin: University of Texas Press, 1992.
1975   "Thought Couplets in Khety's 'Hymn to the Inundation.'" *Journal of Near Eastern Studies* 34:1–29.
1977   *Thought Couplets and Clause Sequences in a Literary Text:* The Maxims of Ptahhotep. Vol. 5. Toronto: Society for the Study of Egyptian Antiquities.
1978   "Some Observations on Pyramid Texts 273–274, the So-Called 'Cannibal Hymn.'" *Journal of the Society for the Study of Egyptian Antiquities* 9: 51–63.
1980   "*Sinuhe:* The Ancient Egyptian Genre of Narrative Verse." *Journal of Near Eastern Studies* 39:89–117.
1988   "'The Shipwrecked Sailor': Prose or Verse? (Postponing Clauses and Tense Neutral Clauses)." *Studien zur altägyptische Kultur* 15:69–109.
1992   *Echoes of Egyptian Voices: An Anthology of Ancient Egyptian Poetry.* Norman and London: University of Oklahoma Press.
1993   *Thought Couplets in* The Tale of Sinuhe. Münchener ägyptologische Untersuchungen 3. Frankfurt am Main: Verlag Peter Lang.
1994   "Oriental Institute Ostracon 25346 (O. Wilson 100)." In *For his Ka: Essays Offered in Memory of Klaus Baer,* edited by David P. Silverman. Studies in Ancient Oriental Civilizations 55. Chicago: The Oriental Institute Press.
1995   "Hymn to Aton." In *Civilizations of the Ancient Near East.* A Scribner's Encyclopedia.

Fox, Michael V.
1985   *The Song of Songs and the Ancient Egyptian Love Songs.* Madison: University of Wisconsin Press.

Gardiner, Alan H.

1931   *The Library of A. Chester Beatty: Description of a Hieratic Papyrus with a Mythological Story, Love-Songs, and Other Miscellaneous Texts.* London: Oxford University Press.

1937   *Late-Egyptian Miscellanies.* Bibliotheca Aegyptiaca VII. Bruxelles: La Fondation Égyptologique Reine Élisabeth.

Gilbert, Pierre

1949   *La Poésie Égyptienne.* 2nd ed. Bruxelles: Fondation Égyptologique Reine Élisabeth.

Golénischchev, M. W.

1927   *Papyrus Hiératiques.* Catalogue général des Antiquités Égyptiennes du Musée Caire, Nos. 58001-58036. Cairo: Institut Française d'Archéologie Orientale.

Griffith, F. L.

1898   *The Petrie Papyri: Hieratic Papyri from Kahun and Gurob (principally of the Middle Kingdom).* London: B. Quaritch.

Grimal, Nicholas

1992   *A History of Ancient Egypt.* Oxford: Blackwell. Translated by Ian Shaw.

Hari, Robert

1985   *La Tombe Thébaine du Père Divin Neferhotep (TT50).* Genève: Éditions de Belles-Lettres.

Helck, Wolfgang

1955–   *Urkunden der 18. Dynastie, Hefte 20-22.* Berlin: Akademie-Verlag.
58

Helck, Wolfgang, and Eberhard Otto, eds.

1975–   *Lexikon der Ägyptologie.* 7 vols. Wiesbaden: Otto Harrassowitz.
92

Hermann, Alfred

1959   *Altägyptische Liebesdichtung.* Wiesbaden: Otto Harrassowitz.

Hornung, Erik.

1982   *Conceptions of God in Ancient Egypt: The One and the Many.* Translated by John Baines. Ithaca: Cornell University Press.

1992   *Idea into Image: Essays on Ancient Egyptian Thought.* Translated by Elizabeth Bredeck. New York: Timken Publishers.

Kemp, Barry J.

1989   *Ancient Egypt: Anatomy of a Civilization.* London: Routledge.

Kitchen, K. A.

1975–   *Ramesside Inscriptions Historical and Biographical.* 8 vols. Oxford: B. H. Blackwell.
90

Lichtheim, Miriam
1945   "The Songs of the Harpers." *Journal of Near Eastern Studies* 4:178–
        212, Pls. I–VII.
1973–   *Ancient Egyptian Literature.* 3 vols. Berkeley: University of Califor-
80   nia Press.
Mariette, A.
1872   *Les Papyrus Égyptienne du Musée Boulaq* II. Paris: A. Franck.
Martin, Geoffrey Thorndike
1989   *The Memphite Tomb of Horemheb Commander-in-Chief of
        Tut'ankhamun. I: The Reliefs, Inscriptions, and Commentary.* Fifty-
        Fifth Excavation Memoir. London: Egypt Exploration Society.
Morenz, Siegfried
1973   *Egyptian Religion.* Translated by Ann E. Keep. London: Methuen
        and Co. Original edition, 1960.
Moret, A.
1931   *Bulletin de l'Institut Français d'Archéologie Orientale* 30:725–30 and
        Pls. I–III.
Müller, W. M.
1899   *Die Liebespoesie der alten Ägypter.* Leipzig: J. C. Hinrichs.
Murnane, William J.
1995   *Texts from the Amarna Period in Egypt.* SBL Writings from the
        Ancient World Series 5. Atlanta: Scholars Press.
Naville, Edouard
1886   *Das ägyptische Totenbuch der XVIII. bis XX. Dynastie.* 3 vols. Berlin:
        A. Asher & Co. Reprinted 1971.
Posener, G.
1938–   *Catalogue des Ostraca Hiératique Littéraire de Deir el Médineh.* 3 vols.
80   Cairo: Institut Français d'Archéologie Orientale.
Pritchard, James B.
1955   *Ancient Near Eastern Texts Relating to the Old Testament.* 2nd ed.
        Princeton: Princeton University Press. Egyptian texts translated by
        John A. Wilson.
Sandman, Maj
1938   *Texts from the Time of Akhenaten.* Bibliotheca Aegyptiaca VIII. Brux-
        elles: Fondation Égyptologique Reine Élisabeth.
Sethe, Kurt
1908   *Die altägyptischen Pyramidentexte.* 4 vols. Leipzig: J. C. Hinrichs Ver-
        lag. Reprint, Hildesheim: Georg Olms, 1969.
1927–   *Urkunden der 18. Dynastie.* Urkunden des ägyptische Altertums IV.
30   2nd ed., 4 vols. Berlin: Akademie-Verlag. Reprinted 1961.

1933   *Urkunden des alten Reichs.* Urkunden des ägyptischen Altertums I. 2nd ed. Leipzig: J. C. Hinrichs.

Shafer, Byron E., ed.

1991   *Religion in Ancient Egypt: Gods, Myths, and Personal Practice.* Ithaca: Cornell University Press.

Silverman, David P., ed.

1994   *For His Ka: Essays Offered in Memory of Klaus Baer.* Studies in Ancient Oriental Civilizations 55. Chicago: Oriental Institute Press.

Simpson, William Kelly, R. O. Faulkner, and Edward F. Wente, Jr.

1973   *The Literature of Ancient Egypt.* 2nd ed. New Haven: Yale University Press.

Smith, W. Stevenson, and William Kelly Simpson

1981   *The Art and Architecture of Ancient Egypt.* 2nd ed. The Pelican History of Art. New York: Penguin Books Ltd. Original edition, 1958.

Trigger, B. J., B. J. Kemp, D. O'Connor, and A. B. Lloyd

1983   *Ancient Egypt: A Social History.* Cambridge: Cambridge University Press.

Tylor, J. J., and F. Ll. Griffith

1894   *The Tomb of Paheri at El Kab.* Eleventh Memoir. London: Egypt Exploration Fund. [Bound with Edouard Naville, *Ahnas el Medineh Heracleopolis Magna*]. Reprinted 1981.

Van der Plas, Dirk

1986   *L'Hymn à la Crue du Nil.* 2 vols. Leiden: Nederlands Instituut voor het Nabije Oosten.

Wente, Edward F.

1980   Translations in The Epigraphic Survey, *The Tomb of Kheruef: Theban Tomb 192.* Oriental Institute Publications 102. Chicago: The Oriental Institute of the University of Chicago.

Žabkar, Louis V.

1988   *Hymns to Isis in Her Temple at Philae.* Hanover: Brandeis University Press.

Zandee, J.

1947   *De Hymnen aan Amon van Papyrus Leiden I 350,* recto. Oudheidkundige Mededelingen uit het Rijksmuseum van Oudheded, New Series XXVIII. Leiden: Het Rijksmuseum van Oudheden.

Glossary

Abdju-fish. Unidentified fish, usually mentioned in the context of Rê's journey in the Night Bark and accompanied by the *int*-fish (the bulti-fish). Watches for the appearance of Apophis.

Abu. The town of Elephantine in the far south of Egypt proper, near the present-day city of Aswan. Source of stone for monuments and the collecting point for ivory from the south.

Abydos. Religious center for ancient Egypt. Site of the burials of the earliest Egyptian kings; traditional place for the grave of Osiris, whose city it is. Destination for pilgrimages by both the living and the dead.

Afterworld. Translation of Egyptian word *duat*, the realm that the individual reaches at death. Also translated as "otherworld" or "underworld."

Akhenaton [Akhenaten]. (1350–1334 B.C.E.). One of the last kings of Dynasty 18. First known monotheist; a heretic according to traditional Egyptian religion.

Amarna. City in Middle Egypt, about halfway between Giza and Thebes, built by King Akhenaton for the worship of his god, Aton.

Ameneminet. Official during the reign of Merenptah. Dynasty 19, end of 13th century B.C.E. Several of his letters to Pentaweret survive on Papyrus Sallier I.

Amenmose. "Overseer of the cattle of Amun." Lived during Dynasty 18. Owner of stele known as Louvre Stele 286 on which appears the most extensive account of the Osiris myth known from pharaonic (as opposed to Greek) times.

Amun [Amon]. Chief deity of Egypt from the Middle Kingdom on. Originates in Thebes and becomes prominent when his devotees, the

184

princes of Thebes, unite a divided Egypt and become the pharaohs of Dynasties 11 and 12. He is "the Hidden One."

Amun-Rê [Amon-Rê]. The supreme god of New Kingdom Egypt, King of the Gods, expressed as a fusion of the divine personalities of Amun (The Hidden One) and Rê (the ancient and highly visible sun god).

Andjeti. "He of the town of Andjet." An early god of the Delta at Busiris. Precursor of Osiris.

Ani. Owner of one of the finest and fullest copies of *The Book of the Dead.* Lived at the end of Dynasty 18.

Anubis. God of embalming and the necropolis, often portrayed as a jackal.

Apis. Bull-god of Memphis, whose worship goes back to the first dynasties of Egypt. Connected with Ptah, prime god of Memphis.

Apophis [Apep]. Cosmic serpent of disorder, which attacks Rê during his journey in the Night Bark. The battle between Apophis and the followers of Rê occurs nightly; he is constantly defeated but cannot be annihilated. Should he be victorious, the universe would slide back to chaos. Hence the significance of the morning songs to the rising Sun.

Asiatics. General term for the peoples east and northeast of Egypt. Often pejorative.

Astarte. Syro-Palestinian goddess of war. Reaches Egypt during the New Kingdom and functions as a protector of horses and chariotry.

Atef. See **Crowns.**

Aton [Aten]. The god conceived of by the monotheistic King Akhenaton (1350–1334 B.C.E.). A version of the traditional Egyptian sun-god, manifesting himself in the light and warmth of the sun's disk.

Atum. The original creator and sun-god according to the theology of Heliopolis. He created the Ennead, the conclave of the Nine Great Gods, which constituted the central pantheon of ancient Egypt.

Atum-Horakhty. Atum as he was identified and fused with Horus of the Two Horizons, the figure of the rising sun of the new day. In this conception, Rê himself was the sun as seen during the major part of the day and Atum was the old, or setting, sun.

Atum-Khepri. Atum as he was identified with the cosmic scarab beetle (Kheprer or Khepri) pushing the sun across the sky.

Aye. Member of the royal family toward the end of Dynasty 18. He became king for a short time (1325–1321 B.C.E.) following the death of Tutankhamun, preceding General Horemheb, who restored Egypt to its traditional ways. Aye's Amarna tomb contains the finest copy of Akhenaton's "Hymn to Aton."

Ba. One of the major aspects of the human personality, according to the ancient Egyptians. In this book, translated as "spirit," in order to distinguish it from the *ka*, which is translated as "soul."

Ba-en-rê. "Spirit of Rê." The prenomen of King Merenptah of Dynasty 19 (1212–1202 B.C.E.).

Baboon. Animal sacred to Thoth, who at times is portrayed as a baboon. The creature is often shown with its arms raised worshiping the morning sun.

Babylon, Ancient. The town of *Hry-aha*, just south of ancient Heliopolis. Not the Mesopotamian city.

Bark of Millions of Years. Name of the Night Bark, Rê's skyship, in which he traverses the underworld at night to be ready to rise at the next dawn.

Bark of Rê. The Night Bark or the Day Bark, depending on the context.

Battle of Kadesh. Battle fought by Ramesses II in his fifth regnal year (1275 B.C.E.) against the Hittites at the town of Qadesh (Kadesh) on the Orontes River in Syria-Palestine. It was, in effect, a defeat for the Egyptian forces; but the personal valor of the king was celebrated in a kind of mini-epic poem, "The Battle of Kadesh," which survives in many copies, both on papyri and on monuments.

Becoming. Egyptian *kheperu*. The condition or process of coming into being, usually from nothingness. Often a materialization or appearance of a deity. The cosmos "becomes" when Atum creates it.

Bee. The heraldic creature of Lower Egypt, the Delta.

Benben. A sacred stone in the shape of a squat obelisk in the temple at Heliopolis. It was thought to represent the initial form of the sun god when he first rose out of chaos (*Nun*) on the hillock from which he created the universe.

Beyond. A translation for the place of the afterlife.

Black Land. A designation for Egypt, especially the black soil of its fertile valley. A reference to terrain, not to people.

Book of the Dead. The collection of religious spells, hymns, and prayers gathered in New Kingdom Egypt and divided into the chapters of a kind of "book." Egyptians who could afford it would select the chapters that appealed to them. A copy was buried with them and used as a guide to the afterworld.

Bull of Heaven. The strength and virility of the bull personified as a cosmic being.

Bull of Heliopolis. The Mnevis, ancient sacred bull of Heliopolis, especially prominent in the New Kingdom and later. Mediator for the sun-god; source of oracles.

Bulti-fish. Translation for the Egyptian *int*-fish. See **Abdju-fish.**

Busiris. Ancient town in the middle of the Delta, "House of Osiris." Reputed to be the birthplace of the god.

Buto. Ancient town in the western Delta, figuring primarily in religious texts. Known as Pê, the mythical capital of the prehistoric northern kingdom before the unification by King Menes ca. 3100 B.C.E.

Cartouche. The elongated oval in which the fourth and fifth names (the prenomen and nomen) of the king's titulary are written.

Celestial Cow. A goddess of the heavens who aids the deceased king in attaining his proper place in the Beyond.

Celestial Ferryman. In the Pyramid Texts, the figure who is to row the transfigured king to his new life in the Beyond.

Chaos. The original formlessness of things before creation (Egyptian, *Nun*). It was, in fact, characterized as a tempestuous watery darkness.

Coming Forth. The emergence of the deceased from the tomb after death as an invisible but vital spirit upon earth. In effect, that person's resurrection.

Council of the Thirty. A high judicial body.

Crocodile. The creature that often signifies death.

Crowns. There were several worn on various occasions by the king. There was the White Crown of Upper Egypt (the South); the Red Crown of Lower Egypt (the North); the Double Crown, a combination of the first two, which signified the union of the Two Lands; the *atef*-crown, a version of the White Crown with two feathers at the sides, first worn by Osiris; the Blue Crown (the *khepresh*), worn in battle; and others.

Darius. Persian king who reigned over Egypt (521–486 B.C.E.), Dynasty 27.

Day Bark. The skyship used by Rê while crossing the heavens during the day.

Day of Mooring. Day of death.

Debty [Djebaty]. "The god in his coffin." Epithet of Osiris and other gods.

Dedja. Unidentified place or building.

Delta. Northern or Lower Egypt (essentially that portion north of modern Cairo), where the Nile fanned out into several branches in antiquity. Site of an independent kingdom in prehistoric times. With the southern portion, the Valley, it forms the Two Lands.

Demaa. Unidentified place or building.

Denderah. Egyptian town just north of Thebes, sacred to Hathor, whose Ptolemaic temple there is one of the best preserved in Egypt.

Divine Tribunal. Name for the Ennead sitting in conclave to administer justice.

Divine Youth [Divine Child]. Rê as the dawn sun, after he has gone below the horizon and been rejuvenated during the night so as to reappear renewed and youthful in the morning.

Djed-pillar. A pole or pillar of uncertain origin serving as a symbol of power. "Stability," "endurance."

Djehuty. Name for the god Thoth.

Djoser [Zoser]. (2737–2717 B.C.E.). King of Dynasty 3 and owner of the Step Pyramid at Saqqara, which was designed by his famous architect Imhotep.

Duamutef. One of the four gods protecting the canopic jars with the deceased's internal organs. Duamutef protected the stomach.

Eastern Horus. Horus as the morning sun and thus protector of lands to the east of Egypt.

Easterners. Here, deities or the blessed dead who have gone to the East, in death, and rise again like Rê to renewed life.

Eight Great Gods. The Ogdoad of Hermopolis, consisting of four pairs of male-female principles (frog- and snake-headed) representing the receptacle for the cosmos, darkness, space, and incipient motion.

El-Hibis. Locale in the Kharga Oasis in the western desert. Site of the Hibis Temple dedicated to Amun by Darius I (521–486 B.C.E.).

El-Kab. Town in southern Egypt about halfway between Thebes (Luxor) and Elephantine (Aswan). Home of the tutelary goddess of Upper Egypt, Nekhbet.

Elder Horus. The ancient cosmic Horus, "whose right eye is the sun and whose left is the moon." Not Horus the son of Isis and Osiris.

Elephantine. City at the south of Egypt, near the present city of Aswan.

Enemy. Epithet for Apophis, the cosmic serpent of disorder.

Ennead. The Nine Great Gods of the Heliopolitan cosmology. Atum, the creator god (later, Rê) formed Shu (air) and Tefnut (moisture), who united to produce Geb (earth) and Nut (sky), who in turn produced the four deities of the Osirian cycle: Osiris, Isis, Nephthys, and Seth.

Enneads, Two. The Greater and the Lesser. The Greater consists of the nine gods of the Heliopolitan cosmology, while the Lesser stems from Horus, child of Isis and Osiris. When the two are spoken of together, all gods of the Egyptian pantheon are meant.

Esna. City south of modern Luxor. Site of the ptolemaic Temple of Khnum.

Euphrates. The great waterway of Mesopotamia.

Evil One. Epithet for Apophis, the cosmic serpent of disorder.

Eye. One of the most potent symbols for the power of destruction and healing known to ancient Egypt. Originally the left eye (the moon) of the god Horus; it was torn out by Seth and restored by Thoth (the *wedjat-eye*), becoming a potent symbol of protection. In another of the myths, the Eye simply leaves in anger and needs to be recovered, its anger being conveyed by its retributive and punishing power. Hathor, for instance, goes down from heaven as the Eye to destroy mankind, which had plotted mischief against Rê.

Eye of Horus. The Eye, especially as torn out by Seth and restored by Thoth.

Eye of Mut, Eye of Atum, etc. The Eye as it serves various gods, either in a protective or retributive capacity.

Faiyum. A lush region in middle Egypt with a lake and fertile fields. It was particularly prominent during Dynasty 12 and the Ptolemaic Period.

Falcon. Personification of the cosmic Horus, the prime Upper Egyptian deity of predynastic times. His worship was centered in Hierakonpolis.

Falcon-gods, Two. Possibly Horus and Seth, with "falcon" in this context meaning "royal." Their enmity needs to be pacified by Maat.

Field of Offerings. Egyptian *Sekhet Hetepu.* Dwelling place of the gods and the blessed dead in the Afterworld.

Field of Reeds. Egyptian, *Sekhet Iaru.* Along with the *Sekhet Hetepu,* the dwelling of the blessed dead.

First Occasion. The time of the creation.

First Time. Creation.

Followers of Horus. The deified rulers of predynastic Hierakonpolis. Sometimes, the blessed dead.

Foremost of the Westerners. Epithet of Osiris.

Form. Translation of the Egyptian word *kheperu.* The materialization, appearance, or incarnation of a deity. It is the visible presentation of an invisible power.

Geb. Earth as a god, personified as male. He was the consort of Nut, the sky, and father of Osiris, Isis, Nephthys, and Seth.

God's Father. A priestly title of uncertain meaning but not implying a blood-relationship to the king. Often with reference to a god, that is, "God's Father of Amun."

God's Land. The region to the east of Egypt. Sometimes Punt or the spice-lands, sometimes Sinai or Lebanon.

Golden Horus. Third in the series of the five great names in the royal titulary. Its origin and meaning are still unclear.

Golden One. Epithet especially of Hathor as the goddess of love.

Great Goddess. Epithet of various major goddesses. In Egyptian it is a generic title, *Wrt*, "The Great One."

Great Green Sea. Probably best understood as "the open sea." It seems to have referred to both the Red Sea and the Mediterrean Sea.

Great Shrieker. The cry of the creator god either as a divine falcon or as the celestial goose who laid the egg of the universe.

Great Staircase. The locale in the Afterworld where the blessed congregate to worship Rê or Osiris. The foot of the throne.

Great Wild Bull. A celestial deity in the form of a bull, betokening strength, virility, and engendering power. Divine bulls in various manifestations were worshiped all over Egypt (Apis, Mnevis).

Greatest of Seers. The High Priest of a god, usually of Rê of Heliopolis.

Hall of the Two Truths. The place of the final judgment of the deceased in the Afterworld, where the heart was weighed in the balance against the feather of Maat, or Truth.

Hall of Truth. Apparently the same as the preceding entry.

Hand-of-Shu. Ritual object carried by the priest.

Hapy. (1) The god of the Nile River; personification of the energy that made it rise each year to flood and fertilize Egypt. Egypt is "the gift of the Nile."

Hapy. (2) One of the four gods protecting the canopic jars containing the embalmed internal organs of the deceased. Hapy was responsible for the lungs.

Harper's Songs. A small group of lyric poems found in funerary contexts which express the *carpe-diem* theme, "Seize the day!" They advocate enjoying life while it lasts and not thinking of the inevitability of death. All this runs directly contrary to mainstream Egyptian religious ideas.

Hathor. Many-faceted goddess. Daughter of Rê, a sky-goddess as "house" (womb) of Horus, the high-flying falcon. Also a cow-goddess, generally benign, and the goddess of love.

Heart, Will, Mind. From the Egyptian *ib*. The seat of thinking, feeling, and willing was the same for the ancient Egyptian, and it was the heart. The brain was perceived as having no useful function and was discarded at mummification.

Heliopolis. The earliest great city of ancient Egypt; locale where the theology of the sun-god flourished. Slightly northeast of Giza and Saqqara; now a suburb of modern Cairo.

Herakleopolis. City in Middle Egypt near the Faiyum. Center for the kings of Dynasties 9 and 10 in a divided Egypt during the First Intermediate Period (2213–2010 B.C.E.).

Hermopolis. City in Middle Egypt between the Faiyum and Assiut. City of the god Thoth, who became Hermes in the Greco-Roman period. Also, the source of the Ogdoad, the Eight Great Gods who represented a theology of origins differing from that of Heliopolis.

Hierakonpolis. Ancient *Nekhen*, on the west bank of the Nile in Upper Egypt, opposite el-Kab. Center for worship of the cosmic Horus, the falcon-god, and perhaps the major center of Upper Egyptian late prehistoric and predynastic civilization. The Followers of Horus seem to be the deified predynastic kings from this locale.

Hill of Creation. The mound that rose of itself out of Chaos (*Nun*) and upon which the creator god, Atum, stood to create the universe.

Hor. Brother of Suty and co-owner of a stele with a pre-Amarna sun hymn. Time of Amenhotep III (1386–1349 B.C.E.).

Horakhty. Horus of the Two Horizons, where the sun rose and set. A form of Rê, the sun-god.

Hordjedef. Prince, son of King Khufu (2638–2613 B.C.E.) of Dynasty 4, and one of the sages of ancient Egypt. A fragmentary "Instruction," or wisdom text, reputedly written by him, still exists.

Horemheb. General of the armies during the reign of Tutankhamun. Later becomes the last king (1321–1293 B.C.E.) of Dynasty 18, restoring the traditional ways of Egypt and providing a peaceful bridge to the Ramesside kings of Dynasty 19.

Horizon. Euphemism for the Beyond. One went to or over the Horizon at death.

Horizon-dwellers. The blessed dead, who often come to welcome new arrivals in the Afterworld.

Horus. Very ancient falcon-god, Lord of the Sky and protector of the king. This is the cosmic Horus and is sometimes fused (or confused) with Horus the Child, son of Isis and Osiris. In either conception, one of the greatest gods of Egypt. He is also personified in the reigning king.

Horus of the Horizon. Horakhty.

Horus of Two Horizons. Horakhty.

House of Ptah in Memphis. The Temple of Ptah, which in its heyday was even larger than the Temple of Karnak.

House of the Prince. Ancient building attached to the sun-god's temple at Heliopolis, used for judicial proceedings.

House of the Scepter. The city of *Waset*, that is, Thebes.

House of the Spirit of Ptah. Designation for the great Temple of Ptah at Memphis.

Hu. Here, an epithet for the sun-god. Later, the personification of divine or authoritative speech from the lips of a god or king.

Hunefer. Owner of a funerary papyrus of the Book of the Dead from Thebes. Time of Seti I (1291–1279 B.C.E.) at the beginning of Dynasty 19. Overseer of Seti's temple.

Hypselis. Egyptian *Shashotep,* near Assiut in Middle Egypt. Town of Seth.

Iaru. For "the Field of Reeds," the dwelling place of the blessed dead.

Ibis. A bird sacred to Thoth, whose form the god someimes took. Symbol of Thoth's wisdom and judiciousness.

Igret. Designation for the necropolis and especially for the realm of the dead.

Imhotep. Flourished during the reign of King Djoser (2737–2717 B.C.E.) in Dynasty 3. Architect of the Step Pyramid at Saqqara; physician and sage, author of a book of wisdom (not extant). His reputation became so great that he was deified in later dynasties.

Imsety. One of the four gods protecting the canopic jars containing the embalmed internal organs of the deceased. Imsety was responsible for the liver.

Imy-Kehau. "The Raging One," an otherworld deity.

Inherkhawy. Foreman of one of the teams working on the royal tombs in the Valley of the Kings; living at Deir el-Medineh. Time of Ramesses III and IV (early 12th century B.C.E.), Dynasty 20.

Int-fish. The bulti-fish. With the abdju-fish accompanies and protects the Night Bark of Rê against Apophis.

Intef [Inyotef]. Name for kings of both Dynasties 11 and 17. The name is attached to the fine Harper's Song appearing on Papyrus Harris 500.

Ipet-Sut. Egyptian *Ipt-Swt.* Name for the Temple of Karnak, the center of religious consciousness and activity in New Kingdom Egypt.

Isderektiw. Unknown land or people in Syria-Palestine.

Isheru. The precinct of the Temple of Mut in the complex of buildings known as Karnak in Thebes.

Isis. The great mother goddess, wife of Osiris and mother of Horus in the Heliopolitan cosmology, symbolic mother of the king. Has immense supernatural power. When Osiris is murdered by Seth, she gathers the pieces of his dismembered body, reunites them, and accomplishes his resurrection. He then impregnates her with Horus and goes to rule the Kingdom of the Dead. She is central to one of the great myths of death and resurrection.

Island of Fire [Isle of Flames]. The primordial hillock or mound where the sun-god came into being and created (the fire of) light.

Itef-reri. Father of Pahery, Mayor of el-Kab.

Iwn-des. A locality. In the Eastern Desert?

Iwn-mutef. "Pillar of his Mother." Epithet of the young Horus as protector of his mother, Isis; hence, an epithet of the king.

Iyty. "He is come." Pun on the function of Horus, the son, who attends on his departed father, the king, now fused with Osiris.

Jubilee. The *heb-sed* festival celebrating renewal of the king's power and abilities, usually first held after thirty years on the throne and then each three years thereafter.

Justice. *Maat* as the word is translated in judicial or moral contexts. See **Truth.**

Ka. One of the aspects of the ancient Egyptian personality, along with the *ba, akh,* body, shadow, and name. In this book, translated as "soul." Not easily defined, though it seems to function as a kind of "double" of the person, who "goes to his or her *ka*" at death, as if it were waiting for the person in the next world.

Kagabu. A Scribe of the Treasury in Papyrus Anastasi IV, in which he has a short prayer to Amun (No. 74).

Kam. Mother of Pahery, Mayor of el-Kab.

Kamutef. Epithet of both kings and gods, "Strong Bull of his Mother." Used when the virility, strength, or engendering power of the personage is to be emphasized.

Karnak, Temple of. The great complex of buildings at Thebes, constituting the center of Egyptian religious activity from the Middle Kingdom on. Vital for two thousand years.

Kemwer. The Great Black One. The bull of Athribis in the Delta. Also an epithet of Osiris of Athribis.

Khakaurê. Prenomen of King Senusert III (1862–1843 B.C.E.) of Dynasty 12.

Khatti. The land of the Hittites, north of Syria-Palestine, roughly modern Turkey.

Khayt. "She Who Rises in Splendor." Here, a name for Maat, goddess of Truth.

Khenty-menutef. A celestial being who takes the deceased king to Geb. Also, an epithet of Horus.

Kheper. The third, or Golden Horus, name in the royal titulary of Senusert III (1862–1843 B.C.E.) of Dynasty 12.

Khepri. The sun and creator god in scarab-beetle form, thought of especially as the newly rising sun or as the divine beetle which pushes the sun across the sky.

Kheruef. Scribe and Steward of the Great Royal Wife of Amenhotep III, Tiye. Time of Amenhotep III and IV (Akhenaton) in Dynasty 18.

Khety. Author of the "Hymn to the Nile" and other literary works. A Ramesside scribe calls him the greatest of the Egyptian writers. Lived in Dynasty 12.

Khnum. The ram-god and potter-god, who forms creatures on his potter's wheel. He is prominent in the cataract region of the south and regulates the Nile in association with Hapy. Particularly prominent at Elephantine, he also has a major temple at Esna.

Khonsu. Moon god at Thebes. Son of Amun and Mut.

Khor. Egyptian name for Syria-Palestine.

King of the Sedge and the Bee. Epithet of the king, introducing his fourth name in the royal titulary, the Nomen or *nsw-bit* name.

Kush. Egyptian name for the countries directly to the south of Egypt, that is, Nubia.

L.p.h. Abbreviation for the English translation of the phrase that usually follows mention of the king's name, "live, prosper, be healthy."

Lake of Horus. Unidentified. In his "Hymn to the Rising and Setting Sun" (No. 39), Ani speaks as if Rê, or Horus, were rising out of chaos to create the world.

Lake of Myrrh. Apparently a locale down the coast of East Africa in or near the land of Punt.

Lake of the Two Knives. A battleground in the sky (where Apophis is defeated?). Also, a lake near Hermopolis.

Land that Loves Silence. The necropolis and the Afterworld.

Lesser Ennead. A second group of nine gods with Horus at their head. When the Greater and the Lesser Enneads are mentioned together, the entire pantheon of Egyptian gods is meant.

Libya. As now, the land to the west of Egypt.

Litany. A hymn or prayer with a refrain repeated at regular intervals.

Lord of Abydos. Osiris.

Lord of All. The supreme deity, usually Atum, Rê, or Amun, depending on the period.

Lord of the Sacred Land. Osiris in his capacity as King of the Dead.

Lord of Thebes. Amun or Amun-Rê.

Lower Egypt. The Delta in the north.

Maat [Ma'at]. The Egyptian word for the root concept of ancient Egyptian civilization, representing a fusion of our concepts of truth, justice, and (both cosmic and civil) order.

Manu, Land of. The region of the setting sun and, by extension, the realm of the dead.

Medjay. Nomadic people from the south, in Nubia, used in the New Kingdom as police and auxiliary troops.

Mehenu. A snake-goddess who, like Nekhbet and Buto (Edjo), functioned as a uraeus to protect the king.

Mehy. Character appearing occasionally in the New Kingdom love songs. High-born or a prince, he seems to function as a pattern or arbiter for lovers.

Memphis. The first great national city of Egypt, southwest of present-day Cairo. It was the capital of the Old Kingdom and extended for miles along the west bank of the Nile.

Merenptah. (1212–1202 B.C.E.). Son and successor on the throne to King Ramesses II in Dynasty 19. With his father, a candidate for "pharaoh of the Exodus."

Merenrê. (2357–2350 B.C.E.). Reigned during Dynasty 6.

Mery-Amun [Mer-Amun]. "Beloved of Amun." An addendum to the Nomen of both Ramesses II and Merenptah of Dynasty 19.

Meryna. Members of the military class in Syria.

Meskhaat. Celestial deity who assists Rê in finding a place for the newly arrived king.

Min. God of fertility and sexual procreativity. Ithyphallic.

Min-Amun. Fusion of the sexual abilities of Min with the person of the supreme deity.

Miscellanies. New Kingdom anthologies, generally of schoolboy pieces or pieces written by scribes in training. Filled with hymns, prayers, eulogies, bits of wisdom, and snippets of history, usually with a decided slant to "improve" the young student's desire to enter the scribal profession.

Mistress of Heaven. Epithet of various goddesses, notably Mut, Hathor, and Isis.

Montu. God of war, arising in Thebes with the appearance of the Middle Kingdom (ca. 2040 B.C.E.).

Mut. Goddess of Thebes. At times portrayed as a lioness or cat. Consort of Amun and mother of Nefertem, god of the blue lotus. Has a major function as a mother-goddess and protector of the king.

Mut-hotepet. Owner of a funerary papyrus of the Book of the Dead. Probably Dynasty 20.

Mysteries. Translation for Egyptian word, *shetau*, "secret things" or "religious mysteries."

Nakht. Royal scribe and "general of the army"; owner of a funerary papyrus of the Book of the Dead. Probably Dynasty 20.

Name. An aspect of the Egyptian personality. Much more significant than the word implies today. Almost "reputation" or "character"; what others think of one.

Naref. Unknown locality connected with Osiris.

Naunet. Female counterpart of Nun, the primal chaos; member of the Ogdoad in the Herakleopolitan cosmology. Also, personification of the counter-heaven.

Nebmaatrê. Prenomen of Amenhotep III (1386–1349 B.C.E.) of Dynasty 18. Father of Akhenaton. His court was possibly the most splendid in all Egyptian history.

Necropolis. Term for the Egyptian cemetery, "the City of the Dead," which was indeed laid out with streets and "houses of eternity."

Nefer-kheperu-rê Wa-en-rê. The prenomen and nomen in the royal titulary of King Akhenaton (1350–1334 B.C.E.).

Nefer-neferu-aton. Name of Queen Nefertiti, the Great Royal Wife of Akhenaton.

Neferhotep. Priest of Amun-Rê ("God's Father") and owner of Theban Tomb 50 in the necropolis of Western Thebes. Time of Horemheb (1321–1293 B.C.E.).

Neferkarê. Pepi II (2350–2260 B.C.E.), late Dynasty 6. Reigned almost one hundred years.

Nefertiti. Queen and wife of Akhenaton (1350–1334 B.C.E.). Major figure of the Amarna Period.

Nefrus. Girlfriend of the speaker of the love poem.

Nehebu-kau. "He who awards distinction." Designation of various divinities, especially of the sun-god.

Nekhbet. Vulture goddess of el-Kab. Mistress of the White Crown of Upper Egypt and protectress of the king.

Nemes. A royal headdress or head-cloth of striped material fitting tightly over the head and lapping over the shoulders.

Nenet. Variant of Naunet, female counterpart of Nun; the counter-heaven.

Nephthys. Youngest goddess of the Osirian generation in the Heliopolitan cosmology, sister of Osiris, Isis, and Seth. Functions mainly as a mourner for the deceased, usually as paired with Isis.

Nepri. The grain-god, personification of the grain. An epithet or a version of Osiris.

Netcherkheperu. The first, or "Horus," name of King Senusert III (1862–1843 B.C.E.) of Dynasty 12.

Netchermesut. The second, or "Two Ladies," name of Senusert III (1862–1843 B.C.E.) of Dynasty 12.

Night Bark. The ship used by Rê for his nightly journey through the afterworld.

Nine Bows. Metonymy for the peoples traditionally thought of as subjugated by the king of Egypt.

Nine Great Gods. The Ennead of Heliopolis created by the sun-god Atum.

Nine Peoples. Those traditionally thought of as subjugated by the king of Egypt.

NN. Designation for a proper name to be added later, usually in either the Book of the Dead or the Pyramid Texts.

Nu. Variant of Nun, the primal chaos personified.

Nubia. Region adjoining Egypt to the south.

Nun. The original watery abyss prior to creation. "Chaos."

Nut. The sky-goddess of the Heliopolitan cosmology. Consort to Geb, the earth, and mother of the Osirian generation of gods.

Ogdoad. The conclave of the Eight Great Gods of Hermopolis. Conceived as male-female pairs (frog- or snake-headed) representing the receptacle for the cosmos, space, darkness, and incipient motion.

Orion. The constellation personified as a major astral deity. He is obsured by the dawn and reappears at night.

Osiris. One of the greatest of the Egyptian gods, betokening resurrection after death. His reanimation, through the good offices of his sister/wife Isis, after his murder and dismemberment by his jealous brother Seth, became the promise to all Egyptians that they would, after death, continue existence in a happy eternal life in the company of Osiris himself.

Osiris, An. As early as the Old Kingdom the concept developed that the Egyptian, at death, would live again in the Beyond. That is, he would reenact the death and resurrection of the god Osiris. In doing so, he became an osiris.

Pahery. Scribe of the Treasury and Mayor of el-Kab and Esna, living in earlier Dynasty 18 (the earlier fifteenth century B.C.E.). The inscription in his tomb gives the fullest surviving description of what life in the next world was thought to be like.

Pentaweret. Correspondent with the treasury official Amenemimet. Reign of Merenptah, Dynasty 19, late thirteenthth century B.C.E. Several of the letters between the two have survived in Papyrus Sallier I.

Pepi. There were actually two kings of Dynasty 6 with this name, Pepi I (2395–2360 B.C.E.) and Pepi II (2350–2260 B.C.E.). Both had Pyramid Texts carved in their tombs.

Peqer. The precinct of Osiris at Abydos where the god was thought to be buried and where his festival was celebrated.

Per-new Shrine. Along with *pr-nsr*, the national shrine of Lower Egypt at Buto.

Per-nezer Shrine. Along with *pr-nw*, the national shrine of Lower Egypt at Buto.

Per-wer Shrine. The national shrine of Upper Egypt at el-Kab.

Phoenix. The *benu*-bird of Heliopolitan religion, connected to the sun-god Rê and the *benben*-stone in the temple there. Also identified with the *ba*-bird, representing the "spirit" or "soul." Long-lived, it reconstituted itself from its ashes, thus becoming a symbol of renewal and figuring in the king's *sed*-festival or Jubilee.

Place of Fire. Unknown; perhaps the redness of the dawn thought of as fire and a place of judgment (from the context).

Place of Truth. General designation for holy places, but specifically the necropolis of western Thebes and Deir el-Medineh.

Pomegranate Tree. The sacred tree honored in Herakleopolis.

Ptah. The creator god of Memphis, who thought out and spoke the creation into existence. A competitor to Atum and Rê of Heliopolis (himself creating the sun), though in both cases the remainder of the cosmology was the same. A cosmic universal god, but also god of crafts and craftsmen. He coalesces with Tatenen.

Ptah-Sokar. Ptah in his particular identification with the Memphite necropolis.

Punt. A mysterious and romantic country south on the east coast of Africa, source of exotic commodities during pharaonic times. Often invoked in the love songs.

Pyramid Texts. A series of hieroglyphic religious inscriptions carved and painted in the burial chambers of several kings of Dynasties 5 and 6. They comprised hymns, prayers, spells, and incantations dealing with the resurrection of the dead pharaoh.

Qebehsenewef. One of the four gods protecting the canopic jars containing the internal organs of the deceased. He was responsible for the intestines.

Qedem. "The Eastern Country," that is, Syria-Palestine.

Qenna. Merchant and owner of a funeray papyrus of the Book of the Dead.

Raiyt. Goddess of the sun; female counterpart of Rê.

Ramesses II. (1279–1212 B.C.E.) at the beginning of Dynasty 19. Prolific builder and one of the great kings of ancient Egyptian history.

Ramesses III. (1182–1151 B.C.E.) at the beginning of Dynasty 20. Last great pharaoh of Egypt.

Rê. The supreme god, the major name of the sun-god through most of Egyptian history.

Rê-Atum. Rê as he coalesces with the older sun-god, Atum, the original creator god in the cosmology of Heliopolis. Also, Rê as he ages toward sundown in his daily journey across the sky.

Rê-Horakhty. Rê as he is conceived of as the vigorous rising sun of the new day, coalescing with Horakhty, Horus of the Two Horizons.

Rebel. Epithet for Apophis.

Residence. The capital of Egypt; site of the court and royal palace.

River. The Nile, the only river in Egypt.

Ro-geese. A species of goose.

Rosetau. Place-name denoting "the opening of the paths," the gateway to the realm of the dead. The necropolis.

Saamu-plants. Unidentified species of plant. Used medically.

Sa-mehyt. "Son of the Northwind," a pun on Sinuhe's name ("Son of the Sycamore") in the Middle Kingdom narrative *The Tale of Sinuhe*.

Sacred Land. First, the burial ground or necropolis of a town; but more generally, the afterworld or underworld, ruled by Osiris.

Sakhmet. "The Mighty One," daughter of Rê and goddess in the holy family of Memphis; her consort was Ptah and their child was Nefertem. Often portrayed as lion-headed, with the fierceness of the lion, often serving as goddess of pestilence.

Scarab. A species of beetle which is often seen rolling a ball of dung as a food supply. Taken as an image of Kheprer, the cosmic Beetle, pushing the sun across the sky. Cut from various stones, the image served for use as amulets and seals, the latter often with hieroglyphic commemorations on their reverse.

Sedge. The Egyptian reed plant. A heraldic symbol for Upper Egypt.

Sem-priest. One of the categories of priest dealing with the burial of the dead and serving in various rituals and festival processions.

Senusert I. (1943–1899 B.C.E.). Second king of Dynasty 12. The reigning pharaoh for *The Tale of Sinuhe*.

Senusert III. (1862–1843 B.C.E.). Fifth king of Dynasty 12.

Serpent. The cobra-goddess appearing as the uraeus on the brow of the king, protecting him and destroying his enemies.

Serpents, Two. The double uraeus, perhaps signifying the protective goddesses of both Upper and Lower Egypt (Nekhbet and Wadjet) and serving the same function as the single cobra-goddess.

Seth. God of confusion, the desert wastes, and foreign lands. Son of Geb and Nut, murderer of his brother, Osiris. Rival of Horus for rule of the land of Egypt. He is judged the loser by the Grand Tribunal of the Ennead, and Horus is awarded the Two Lands. Like Apophis, often represents a principle of confusion and disorder. Often portrayed in the shape of an unknown desert beast with long triangular ears and upright tail.

Seti I. (1291–1279 B.C.E.). Reigned early in Dynasty 19; father of Ramesses II.

Shade. Part of the individual's personality. Not easily translated, but something like the shadow or ghost of a person.

Shedeh. A kind of wine.

Sherden. A people from the Mediterranean ("Peoples of the Sea"), active ca. 1400–1200 B.C.E., attacking Egypt from outside and later serving in Ramesside armies. Perhaps connected with Sardinia.

Shetyt. The precinct of Sokar, god of the Memphite necropolis.

Shezemu. A god of butchering and execution, on the one hand, and of wine and aromatic oils, on the other.

Shrine of the North. Per-nezer at Buto.

Shrine of the South. Per-wer at el-Kab.

Shu. God of air in the Heliopolitan cosmology; one of the first two deities (along with Tefnut) created by Atum, the creator god.

Sidelock-Wearers. Four male divinities of the eastern sky who aid the king in his resurrection.

Sinai. The desert region east of Egypt across the Red Sea. In pharaonic times, a mining region and site of major copper mines.

Sinuhe. Title character in one of the finest ancient Egyptian works of fiction. A highly placed royal official who flees into exile under threat of a coup against his sovereign, Senusert I, he spends his life in Syria-Palestine recovering his self-respect and is finally welcomed back into the royal family by his benevolent king.

Sokar. God of the necropolis at Memphis, hawk-headed. Seems to function, like Osiris, as symbolizing the resurrection from death.

Son of Nut. Usually designates Seth rather than Osiris.

Son of Sothis. Sopedu, a god of the northeast Delta. Earlier, in the Pyramid Texts, the child of Sothis and the resurrected king.

Sons of Horus. The four gods protecting the embalmed internal organs of the deceased: Imsety, Hapy, Duamutef, and Qebehsenewef.

Sothis. Goddess of Sirius, the Dog Star. Its heliacal rising foretold the rising of the Nile and the coming inundation (the New Year).

Soul. In this book, translating the Egyptian word *ka*. A main component of the personality, in addition to the *ba*, *akh*, shade, body, and name.

Souls of Heliopolis [of Iwnw]. Deified predynastic rulers of the ancient religious center of sun worship.

Souls of Nekhen. Deified predynastic rulers of the southern kingdom, the living king's ancestors as protectors.

Souls of Pê. Deified predynastic rulers of the northern kingdom, the living king's ancestors as protectors.

Southern Harîm. Designation for Luxor Temple in Thebes.

Spirit. In this book, translating the Egyptian word *ba*. A main component of the personality, in addition to the *ka*, *akh*, shade, body, and name.

Staff-of-life-plants. Designation for edible plants.

Sunfolk. The blessed dead, thought of as in the retinue of Rê, the sun-god.

Suty. One of the brothers, along with Hor, owners of a stele with a hymn to the sun which shows some parallels of phrase to the Amarna hymns of the next generation. Time of Amenhotep III (1386–1349 B.C.E.).

Syria. Designation for the more northern portion of ancient Syria-Palestine (Egyptian *khor*).

Ta-djeser. "The Sacred Land" or the necropolis, especially of Abydos.

Ta-mery. "The Beloved Land," that is, Egypt.

Ta-wer. The district or nome of This and Abydos.

Tatenen. An ancient Memphite god of the fertile land rising out of the Nile flood; coalesces with Ptah as a creator god.

Tayt. Goddess of weaving, especially for the cloth with which to wrap the mummified body.

Tefnut. Goddess of moisture; one of the first beings (along with Shu) made by the creator god, Atum. She and her consort are the first to represent the concepts of male and female in the cosmos.

Teti. (2407–2395 B.C.E.). First king of Dynasty 6 in the Old Kingdom. Represented by a pyramid at Saqqara.

Thebes. One of the two greatest cities of ancient Egypt (along with Memphis), capital during the early Middle Kingdom and throughout the New Kingdom. At the site of modern Luxor in southern Egypt.

This. Capital city of Egypt during the first two dynasties, the Thinite. Near Abydos.

Thoth. God of scribes, knowledge, writing and computation, and guardian of the holy writings. Himself scribe of the Ennead. A moon god who is often portrayed as a baboon or an ibis. Connected with Hermopolis and the Ogdoad.

Transfigured Spirits. Translating the Egyptian word *akhu*, the transfigured or "enlightened" souls of the dead as they appear in all their glory in the afterlife.

True of Voice. The deceased is judged "true of voice" or "vindicated" ("justified") once he or she has passed the Last Judgment before Osiris, where the heart is weighed in the balance against the feather of Maat, or Truth. If the good outweighs the evil, the soul is allowed to pass on into the afterlife.

Truth. One of the words used to translate the Egyptian *Maat*, the root concept of ancient Egyptian civilization. It is a very general and fundamental term signifying a fusion of our concepts of "truth," "justice," and "order" (including cosmic harmony), depending on the context. The (proper) Way.

Twin Kites. Egyptian **djerty,** which means both "kite" and "female mourner." The Twin Kites are thus Isis and Nephthys as they mourn, first, Osiris and then any other deceased person.

Two Banks. Designation for Egypt emphasizing the two sides of the Nile River.

Two Ladies. The heraldic goddesses Nekhbet of Upper Egypt and Wadjet of Lower Egypt. They protect both Egypt and the king. On the king's brow they are the Two Serpents of the double Uraeus.

Two Lands. Egypt, seen as the union of the two prehistoric kingdoms of north and south (Lower and Upper Egypt).

Two Sisters. The goddesses Isis and Nephthys, primarily in their capactiy as mourners for the deceased, whether their brother Osiris or any other of the dead.

Unas [Wenis]. (2428–2407 B.C.E.). Last king of Dynasty 5 and the first pharaoh to have religious writings dealing with resurrection (Pyramid Texts) carved in hieroglyphs on the inner walls of his tomb at Saqqara.

Underworld. Translation of Egyptian *duat*; also "afterlife," "otherworld."

Upper Egypt. Southern Egypt, land of the White Crown, *up*-river.

Ur-god. Designation for the original, primal god of creation in the beginning, called by various names at different times, but generally known as Atum.

Uraeus. The cobra-goddess on the brow of the king, protecting him and destroying his enemies.

User-maat-rê. Here, referring to Ramesses II rather than Ramesses III. The former reigned 1279–1212 B.C.E. during Dynasty 19.

User-maat-rê Mer-Amun. Prenomen and Nomen of King Ramesses III (1182–1151 B.C.E.) of Dynasty 20.

Userhat. Name for the Bark of Amun.

Vindicated. Another translation for "true of voice," indicating the deceased has successfully passed the trial of the Last Judgment.

Visible Form. A technical religious term (Egyptian *kheperu*) indicating the manifestation or visible appearance of a deity, an incarnation, whether fleeting or more lasting. One of the incarnations of Akhenaton's deity, Aton, for instance, is the sun.

Vizier. The official who in power is second only to the king and who in effect administers the country.

Wadjet. Cobra-goddess of Buto in Lower Egypt, serving also as the uraeus-goddess.

Waset. A designation for ancient Thebes, particularly the western portion including the necropolis or City of the Dead.

Waters, Your. A phrase used by a suppliant to announce allegiance to the king. To be on his waters means to be under his protection.

Weary-Hearted. Designation for the murdered Osiris, inert and weary in death prior to his resurrection.

Wedjat. The Uninjured Eye of Horus, that is, "The Healthy One." Symbolizes protection and good health.

Weni. An official of Dynasty 6 who lived during the reigns of Kings Teti, Pepi I, and Merenrê. His tomb biography survives and provides a source of information about the later Old Kingdom.

Wennefer. "He Who Was Truly Good" or "He Who Was Perfect." Designation of Osiris.

Wennefer-rê. Osiris in his fusion of power and activity with Rê.

Wenti. The name of a god, here applied to Osiris. "The One who Exists" or "The Triumphant" (over death)?

West. Physically, the City of the Dead; spiritually, the afterlife.

Western Mountain. Manu, the place where the setting sun meets the horizon and where the dead dwell.

Western Souls. The blessed dead.

Westerners. The blessed dead.

White Wall. Epithet of ancient Memphis, enclosed in white walls at the time of its establishment by King Menes, founder of a united Egypt in Dynasty I.

Winding Waterway. A geographical feature of the afterworld.

Yonder. Specifically, the afterworld.

Indexes

(References below are to text numbers, not pages.)

1. Deities

2. Persons

3. Places

Abu, 91
Abydos, 7, 28, 29, 35, 43, 44, 55.i
Afterworld, I, 55.ii, 79
Amarna, II, VI
Asheru, 33.x, 92

Babylon, 44
Beloved Land, 46, 80.i
Below, 32, 41, 43, 45.x
Beyond, 1.viii, 13, 16, 22, 28.iii, 31.iv, 50
Black Land, 60, 64
Busiris, 29, 43, 44, 80.ii
Buto, 31.ii

City of the Wall, 46

Dedja, 23
Delta, 52, 66
Demaa, 23
Denderah, 55.ii
Desert, 27, 28.iii

East, 9
Egypt, 7, 21, 27, 28.ix, 38, 45.vii, 45.x,
    51.i, 51.xiv, 52.ii, 60, 63, 65, 66
El-Kab, VIII, 55.ii
Elephantine, 55.i
Esna, VIII
Euphrates, 33.vi

Faiyum, 52.ix
Field of Offerings, 7, 50
Field of Reeds, 19, 40.v, 43, 50, 55.iii

God's Land, 31.i, 33.vi
Great Green Sea, 31.vii, 33.vi, 45.iv,
    45.ix, 46, 51.x, 55.iv

Hall of Truth, 35
Hall of Two Truths, 28.i, 55.iii
Heaven, 26
Heliopolis, VII, 11, 19, 23, 28.i, 31,
    31.viii, 31.ix, 33.xxx, 33.cc, 33.ccc,
    33.dccc, 35, 37, 43, 44, 48, 50, 53, 65,
    70, 71, 80.ii

Herakleopolis, 28.i, 44
Hermopolis, 28.i, 48, 49, 50, 69, 70
Hierakonpolis, 44
Hill of creation, 23
Horizon, I, 8, 25, 27, 31.ix, 34, 36, 39.i,
    40.ii, 40.iii, 41, 45.i
House of Fire, 72
House of Ptah, 66, 80.ii
House of Ramesses Meramun, 65
House of the Benben, 31.iv, 31.viii
House of the Ka, 33.ccc
House of the Prince, 53, 92
House of the Ruler, 34
House of the Scepter, 59
House of the Spirit of Ptah, 67
Hypselis, 28.i

Iaru, 13
Igret, 38
Ipet-Sut, 30.iii, 31.i, 31.iv, 31.viii, 31.ix,
    32, 33.x
Isderektiw, 63
Island of Fire, 1.iii
Iwn-des, 44

Karnak, 31.ii
Khatti, 66
Khor, 45.vii, 77
Kush, 45.vii

Lake of Horus, 39.ii
Lake of Myrrh, 50
Lake of the Two Knives, 24, 37, 38, 39.ii
Land of the Blessed, 1.x
Land of the Dead, 28.i
Land of Manu, 34
Libya, 61
Lower and Upper Egypt, 51.vi
Lower and upper heavens, 31.i

Manu, 41
Memphis, VII, 33.ccc, 67
Meryna, 63

Naref, 44

4. Subjects

Writings from the Ancient World

Edward F. Wente, *Letters from Ancient Egypt,* 1990.

Harry A. Hoffner, Jr., *Hittite Myths,* 1991; second edition, 1998.

Piotr Michalowski, *Letters from Early Mesopotamia,* 1993.

James M. Lindenberger, *Ancient Aramaic and Hebrew Letters,* 1994.

Martha T. Roth, *Law Collections from Mesopotamia and Asia Minor,* 1995; second edition, 1997.

William J. Murnane, *Texts from the Amarna Period in Egypt,* 1995.

Gary M. Beckman, *Hittite Diplomatic Texts,* 1996.

John L. Foster, *Hymns, Prayers, and Songs: An Anthology of Ancient Egyptian Lyric Poetry,* 1996.

Simon Parker et al., *Ugaritic Narrative Poetry,* 1997.

Printed in the United States
213599BV00001B/57/A

9 780788 501579